BFG3 & ASSOCIATES

BEN GAY III
Salesman • Speaker
Sales Trainer • Consultant

Voice: (800) 248-3555
(530) 622-7777
Fax: (530) 295-9337
E-Mail: bfg3@directcon.net
WWW.BFG3.COM

P.O. Box 2481
Placerville, CA 95667-2481
USA

Getting the People Equation

How to Get the Right People in the Right Jobs and Keep Them

Right

Logan Loomis

To my wife, Rhonda,
without whose support
I couldn't do what I do. I love you.

Acknowledgments

This book would not have been possible without the insights I have gained from the work of Dan Harrison, Ph.D. Thank you Dan for your tireless commitment to provide the reliable, user-friendly and objective data needed to get the right person in the right job. You are not only a scholar, you are a true gentleman. And your work is very cool! To my clients, thank you for having the commitment and faith to apply the principles in this book. I'm blessed to work with courageous, committed and successful leaders. Special thanks to Thomas Mozjesik, Gaylon Hull, Casey Rheinlaender, and John Stedman. To Phillip Christman, thank you Yoda for starting me on the path to understanding the People Equation. You are a great coach and friend. To Abbe O'Rourke, you are the best management thinker I know. Thank you for the support and clarity you contributed. To Nance Guilmartin, thank you my dear friend and colleague for the contribution you have made to my professional and personal development over the years as well as your valuable input. You are the poster child for great situational awareness. To Mike Lee, Dena Lucas, Suzie Hise, Jan Whalen, Scott Roelofs, and Tim Durkin, thank you for contributing your time reading and editing the manuscripts. Your candor and comments are visible. Finally, thank you Benjamin "Dex" Devey for creating a great cover and getting the book ready to publish.

Getting the People Equation Right

How to Get the Right People in the Right Jobs and Keep Them

CONTENTS

PART 1

PART 1

Introduction

The ability to make good decisions regarding
people represents one of the last reliable sources
of competitive advantage since very few
organizations are very good at it.

Peter Drucker

Tom, the CEO of a mid-market IT consulting firm, and
I were having dinner. The diffused lighting in the restaurant, meant to enhance the ambiance, was only contributing
to our somber mood. Tom said, "He's just not working out."
He was talking about Eric, the head of a critical business practice area who—now eight months into the job—was failing.
It was a vitally important hire. We had done everything we
knew to do in order to make a good hiring decision: highly
regarded executive search firm, impressive resume, good story

about his accomplishments, good references and Eric was interviewed by Tom, the CFO, two members of the Board and me. We all liked him. At the end of the interview process we had concluded that Eric was a brilliant guy with great experience. It was clear to us that he had a lot of drive. We were right about his brilliance and drive; but we had all missed something. Something very important.

Tom quickly discovered that Eric alienated those who worked for him by being hyper-critical, demanding and authoritarian. We didn't pick up on that in the interview process. During the interview process we had focused on the results Eric had achieved, his ideas for improvement and his apparent drive to succeed. The references we checked were with senior relationships. Eric apparently managed up very well. To be fair, Tom confirmed that Eric was as brilliant and driven as we thought. He did have great ideas. But it was becoming clear to Tom that morale was declining and that the company was at risk of losing some valued members of the team. Tom had told Eric on several occasions that he was pushing too hard, but, to Tom's frustration, there had been no change in behavior. In the final analysis Tom concluded that Eric was just not going to make it in the job. They parted ways.

If you manage a business you have very likely had similar dinners and parted ways with people you initially thought, for very good reasons, would do a great job. You know the consequences—the significant cost—associated with a hiring mistake. The cost in money, time, productivity and, most of all, in emotional turmoil.

We all know that the goal is to get the right person in the right job. The hard part is how. Certainly no one wants to make hiring mistakes. But there I was talking with Tom about a big mistake. I had to admit to myself after that dinner that I did not have a clear-cut answer on how to consistently get the right person in the right job—how to avoid costly hiring mistakes. I was certainly not new to business. I had practiced corporate law, worked through employment law issues, built executive and sales teams as a CEO in the natural gas industry and been a business advisor to a broad range of companies—and I still did not really know how to consistently get the right person in the right job. My dinner with Tom was certainly not the first time I had discussed people problems with a client. In thinking about it, I realized that I had spent an inordinate amount of time over the years with coworkers, clients and colleagues discussing and working on people problems. It's no doubt the same for you. Despite having legal training on how to handle the consequences of a bad hire, what was needed was training on how to avoid a bad hire. I wondered if there was a clear-cut way to consistently make better hiring decisions and thereby avoid many of the people problems with which we all deal. In the intervening years I've discovered that there is. I call it the *People Equation.*

My goal in working out the People Equation has been to apply the same degree of logic, rigor and strategic insight to hiring decisions that I apply to other business decisions; those involving, for instance, capital, products, services, customers, operations or technology. What has resulted is an analytical framework that has been helpful to the executives and hiring managers with whom I work. This book will share the analytical framework with you in hopes that it will help you make better hiring decisions.

Who is the "you" I'm speaking to? You are the people who are in the trenches day to day trying to get the right person in the right job, develop and satisfy customers and grow the business. Probably like you, I made people decisions for years without a handbook to guide me. I know that's true for most of the businesses I work with. As I began to work out the People Equation, I discovered that there is a tremendous amount of helpful thought capital on the subject. Throughout this book I will cite important critical thinkers and their research that provided fundamental concepts in building the foundation of the People Equation. My goal with this book is to distill into a practical handbook what I've learned through research and real-world application.

The People Equation provides you with a coherent, reliable and consistent analytical framework for making talent decisions—to get the right person in the right job. An executive who has applied the People Equation observes: "It's not only for new hires; it is for promotions and any time you consider moving a person from one job to another—or maybe just changing their duties or tasks. It is about getting a person in the right job and even recognizing when that has not occurred."

The People Equation certainly includes the factors we considered when making the hiring decision for the IT company: experience, education, training, past accomplishments and likability. But, as we found out, these factors alone are not predictive of job success. To get the People Equation right, you need to factor in other considerations that are equally—perhaps more—important in making a talent decision. Other critical factors include:

1. How naturally engaged a person is in his or her work.
2. How effectively a person builds working relationships and makes decisions.

I have framed the People Equation into the following mathematical equation to provide structure and logic:

$$\frac{\text{Key Job Activities}}{(\text{Eligibility} + \text{Suitability})} = \text{High Performance Potential}$$

As you can see from the equation, the ability to make a distinction between job eligibility and job suitability is important for identifying high performance potential. "Eligibility" and "suitability" are likely new terms for you. "Eligibility" is a person's education, training and job experience; what we evaluated for the IT company hire. "Suitability," by contrast, is the degree to which a person's natural tendencies and preferences are aligned with requirements for success in the job. "Eligibility" means that you have the skill and experience needed to do a job; "suitability" means that you have inherent qualities that help you excel in a job. Eligibility and suitability are key concepts in finding a good fit for a job—getting the right person in the right job. The next section will provide you with a deeper understanding of the critically important distinction between eligibility factors and suitability factors. We will then explore each part of the People Equation in depth so that you can effectively use the People Equation in making a talent decision. It is my hope that by the end of this book you will have a new formula for success in making talent decisions. More importantly, I hope this book makes that formula practical and usable.

An Important Distinction

As I began to work out the People Equation I realized that how a person approaches a job is an important factor. Attitude, for instance, is key. Herb Kelleher, former CEO of Southwest Airlines, once said that he started out looking for people with a good attitude.[1] My quandary was, "How do you assess attitude?" I wanted a practical and tangible way of looking at hiring; "attitude" seemed too difficult to describe and too subjective. I experienced a significant breakthrough in my thinking when I was introduced to the work of Dan Harrison, Ph.D.[2] and an important distinction he makes that provides a concrete perspective.

Dr. Harrison has done comprehensive research into job success factors. He makes a distinction between job eligibility factors and job suitability factors. Again, "eligibility" is a person's education, training and job experience; what we evaluated for the IT company hire. "Suitability" is the degree to which a person's natural tendencies and preferences are aligned with requirements for success in the job. Eligibility means that you have the skill and experience to do the job—you can do it. To move beyond mere competence to high performance, you also need to be well-suited for the job: you need the innate qualities that make you right for the job. What is intriguing about Dr. Harrison's research is that it makes those innate qualities tangible and identifiable by basing job suitability on assessable cause-effect theories. Two theories to be exact. The first theory is Enjoyment Performance Theory and the second is Paradox Theory. Let's look at how each of these cause-effect theories provides understanding into how to objectively evaluate suitability traits.

Enjoyment Performance Theory explains that you will perform more effectively in a job if you:

1. Enjoy the tasks required by that job.
2. Have interests that relate to the job.
3. Like the work environment and type of interpersonal interactions involved in and required by the job.

Looking at job performance through the lens of Enjoyment Performance Theory—applying the three criteria—creates a clear-cut framework for assessing a person's attitude and natural aptitude for a particular job. By way of example, let's look at a scene from *The Break-up*, a movie starring Jennifer Aniston and Vince Vaughn.

The two characters are arguing over doing the dishes after a party. She wants him to "want" to help her do the dishes. He bristles back, "Why would I want to do dishes? Why?" That is actually a very important question when evaluating job suitability. Of course Vaughn's character is assuming no one would want to do dishes. In fact, there are people who enjoy doing dishes and have a great attitude when washing dishes. Why? Because they enjoy the tasks involved in cleaning and creating order, they are interested in being physically active and enjoy the opportunity to be in an environment where they can stand and move around. Vince Vaughn's character would not be your guy if you want dishes washed—he's not suitable. Even if he is an expert dish washer with extensive experience, he doesn't want to wash dishes; on an innate level he resists it. We should look for people who "want" to engage in the activities that we need done. Enjoying the activities in a job naturally promotes a good attitude. This is an important concept in the People Equation.

There is another dimension of job suitability that impacts success: situational awareness. Although "situational awareness" can reference a field of study, I am simply using the term to mean how an individual manages his relationship with himself and with others. Is an individual aware of how his actions will impact a situation? Dr. Harrison's application of Paradox Theory to job suitability has helped me understand how to factor a person's situational awareness into a hiring decision. Let me explain.

Paradox Theory recognizes that human beings possess and demonstrate seemingly contradictory traits simultaneously. The paradox is that effectiveness is often the result of a good blending of seemingly contradictory traits. Let's look at communication for example. When we communicate we all—to a lesser or greater extent—possess the qualities of directness and tact. Directness and tact both contribute to effective communication even though they seem to be opposite or contradictory. To be an effective communicator you need to be able to communicate frankly or tactfully *as the situation requires.* If you tend to be more direct than tactful and you encounter a situation that requires tact, you may communicate poorly by being too direct for the situation. Your bluntness may be perceived as rudeness. You are not responding effectively to the situation.

I now understand that a lack of situational awareness was the root of Eric's failure at the IT company. Although Eric's job required him to be authoritative—he needed to make the final decision—he also needed to engage his people in the decision rather than merely direct his people. Therein is the paradox; one that he did not execute well. By not engaging his people he alienated them and diminished his influence, his authority and ultimately his success. He lacked suitability because he was authoritarian rather than managing with a good balance of authority and inclusion.

You will get a deeper understanding of the impact of both Enjoyment Performance Theory and Paradox Theory on job suitability as we explore the People Equation throughout this book. You will also gain insight into how breakthroughs in assessment technology can now give you reliable data on a person's suitability for a particular job. Historically the problem in factoring suitability into a hiring decision has not only been what to evaluate but also how to measure or assess it. As you will see, measuring or assessing suitability is no longer really an issue for businesspeople in light of advances in assessment technology. The state of current assessment technology is one of the most exciting things I can share with you in this book.

Throughout the book you will also gain a deeper understanding of eligibility factors. Both eligibility and suitability are important considerations in evaluating potential job performance. Certainly you cannot be competent in a job without good eligibility. Eligibility means you can do a job. To move beyond mere competence to high performance you also have to factor in suitability. Suitability means you will perform the job because you enjoy the activities required by the job—you want to do it—and that you have the situational awareness to be effective in the job.

———————————— ❦ ————————————

If you can do a job, want to do a job and can respond appropriately to the situations presented by the job, you are creating a formula for success.

———————————————————————

Now that you have been introduced to the basic concepts of suitability and eligibility, let's take a look at the full People Equation.

The People Equation

ELIGIBILITY AND SUITABILITY are key parts of the People Equation. But to get the People Equation right requires evaluating eligibility and suitability in the context of the tasks or activities required by the job. Again, the People Equation can be pictured as follows:

$$\frac{\text{Key Job Activities}}{(\text{Eligibility} + \text{Suitability})} = \text{High Performance Potential}$$

This book will give you insight into each part of the People Equation (key job activities, eligibility and suitability) so that you can put the People Equation to work in making great people decisions.

You will note that the quotient of the People Equation is high performance "potential." In working the People Equation with clients over the last several years, I have found that an additional factor needs to be considered in order to translate high performance "potential" into job success; there is another part to the success formula. The other part of the formula is motivation. The People Equation will tell you whether a candidate can and wants to do a job—is "naturally" motivated to do the work. It addresses the relationship between a person and her job. However, organizations can approach employees in ways that de-motivate. To ensure long-term success you also need to consider the relationship between a person and her manager or the company's culture. When this type of motivation is added to the quotient of the People Equation, the formula for success can be pictured as follows:

High Performance Potential

+ Motivation

_____

Job Success

The late David Ogilvy, a legend in advertising, offers some keen insight into motivation. Ogilvy not only knew what motivated a consumer, he knew what it took to motivate an employee. He understood what it took to both recruit great talent and to realize their potential for Ogilvy & Mather. He wrote, for instance: "When people aren't having fun, they seldom produce good advertising."[3]

Why am I talking about the late David Ogilvy rather than a more contemporary model of motivation? Because he gave me a "wow" moment when I read the following foreword from one of his recruiting brochures:

> "If you join Ogilvy & Mather, we shall teach you everything we know about advertising. We shall pay you well, and do our damnedest to make you succeed. If you show promise, we shall load responsibility on you—fast. Life in our agency can be very exciting. You will never be bored. It's tough, but it's fun. "[4]

I don't think I have ever read a more engaging invitation for a job. He is presenting an opportunity for learning, growth, fun and good compensation. The important thing is that the people who worked for him say that he walked his talk. David Ogilvy had mastered the art of motivation. He used his motivational mastery to build an enduring institution and a vibrant legacy. You can too. This book will show you how to lay a foundation for motivating talent. We will explore how compensation, appreciation and communication, together with creating an opportunity to grow, stretch and have fun, can help you tap into performance potential.

This book will show you ways to succeed in hiring and keeping top performers by showing you how to get the People Equation right and how to develop your motivational competency. Part 1 of the book will break down each individual part of the People Equation. We will first look at the numerator and then at each of the two parts of the denominator. The fourth section—quotient—will bring it all together. Part 2 of the book will look at how to keep your high performers by developing great motivational competency.

Again, it is my hope—and expectation—that by the end of this book you will have a new formula for success in making talent decisions. I am very grateful for the commitment and faith of my clients who have worked with me over the years to get the People Equation right. Throughout the book I share client experiences of the People Equation at work. Because this is intended to be a handbook or field guide, I have chosen not to make those experiences detailed case studies. Rather, I have condensed them into generalized examples. Unless otherwise noted, the names and details have been changed to protect privacy. That also applies to the Tom and Eric encounter that opened the book.

So let's get to it.

People Equation Numerator:
Key Job Activities

Developing Clear Performance Expectations

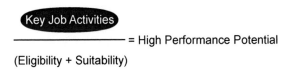

IT TURNS OUT that making a good hiring decision and playing scratch golf have a lot in common. I gained that insight from Mark who is a top salesman for one of my clients. I've gotten to know Mark over the last several years as I have consulted with the sales team for his company. He's an excellent golfer—a scratch golfer. Fortunately that fact surfaced in a conversation rather than by a first hand experience of Mark beating me on the golf course. I was working with the sales team on how to approach a sale. I asked Mark how he approached a hole when he was playing a round of golf. He said, "I start with the hole and then work backwards to the tee." That approach surprised most of the golfers in the room. But it makes sense. Starting with the end in mind is consistent of high performers in any endeavor. Management expert Peter Drucker reminds us that it is the same in business: "The effective executive therefore first makes sure that the job is well-designed."[5] Just like Mark who starts with the hole when he plays golf, start your talent decisions by first understanding the job. For you golfers, I hope Mark's advice also improves your game!

I don't find that many managers heed Drucker's advice and talk in much detail about designing the job itself. To be candid neither did I when I was running a natural gas marketing and trading company. I have learned that the seemingly mundane job description—usually one of the activities a manager most eagerly delegates—is, when properly done, a very potent driver of business success. It is essential for developing clear performance expectations.

Take a look at your job descriptions. If they are like most of the ones I see, they are a laundry list of activities with no clear priority. They don't create clear performance expectations. One way to create clear performance expectations is to follow the advice Larry Bossidy and Ram Charan give in their excellent book *Execution, The Discipline of Getting Things Done*. They advise defining jobs in terms of a few "nonnegotiable criteria" or things a "person *must* be able to do in order to succeed."[6] Defining nonnegotiable activities that must be done in order to succeed creates alignment.

A hiring decision is fundamentally an exercise in alignment. You have to get the right person aligned with the right job. The numerator of the People Equation is about the right job; the denominator is about the right person. The first thing you need to do in order to get the People Equation right is to define the numerator. If you don't have a clear view of what the job is, it is difficult to know who the right person for the job is—it is difficult to consistently achieve alignment.

Fred Smith, CEO and Chairman of FedEx, is quoted as saying, "Alignment is the essence of management."[7] He was discussing alignment in the context of strategic alignment—getting everyone in the company aligned around a company's objectives and corporate philosophy. Although you might not think of crafting a job description as a strategic activity, I invite you to do just that. The concept is not really as far fetched as it might initially seem. Let me explain.

One of the keys to strategic success is the ability to align a strategy to the actions that will drive success. Once a strategic plan is put in place, it is important to ask what activities are required to drive the strategic results for which we are looking. What do we need people to do if the strategy is going to succeed? Job activities are the most elemental building blocks of business performance and, in the final analysis, drive strategic success. Nonnegotiable activities need to be captured in a job description in order to ensure that people are clear about what needs to be done.

Three-step Process for Creating a Strategic Job Description

A straightforward three-step process for creating a "strategic" job description—defining the numerator in the People Equation—is to identify outcomes, nonnegotiable activities and measures. If you were applying for a job wouldn't you want to know exactly what would be expected from you and how your performance would be measured? That's what this process delivers.

Step 1: Define Outcomes

Define the outcomes you expect. As scratch-golfer Mark would say, "Start with the hole and work back."

What does success look like in this particular job? For example, let's say your strategy is to grow revenue ten percent by developing a substantial number of new customers in the coming year. Sales will obviously be a critical job if your strategy is going to succeed. To execute Step 1 you might want to define how much revenue a salesperson needs to generate from new customer sales to achieve ten percent growth.

Step 2: Define Nonnegotiable Activities

Determine what specific sales activities will drive the outcomes you identified in Step 1. Because you want sales revenue from "new customers," one nonnegotiable activity in the sales job itself will be prospecting—identifying and getting in front of potential new customers. Because prospecting is a key strategic job activity, you will want to select people for the job who are effective at prospecting.

Step 3: Define Measures

Decide how you will measure and validate job performance. In the final analysis you will measure the success of prospecting by sales revenue. Sales revenue is, however, a lagging indicator of performance. It's nice to have an early warning sign if prospecting is not going well.

The advantage of defining a specific job activity is that you can measure the activity that drives the outcome you want. "Appointments set" would be an example of a leading measure. Your sales revenue will likely be disappointing if you have not set enough appointments. As the old adage says, "what gets measured gets done." As you define your measures look for leading or driver measurements. That way you can take early corrective action if it is not getting done.

Let's take a look at how sales results improved by identifying and measuring prospecting as a nonnegotiable activity. A life insurance agency contacted me a number of years ago to coach several agents who were good closers but who had problems consistently meeting quota. They were independent agents so they did not have a formal sales manager.

Step 1: What did success look like to these agents? They all wanted to exceed their respective monthly sales quota.

Step 2: What activities were required to do that? To reach and exceed quota they needed to identify and set appointments with a specific number of new prospective clients each week.

Step 3: How would we measure success? The activity was easily measured: you can count the number of referrals generated and contacts made.

When reviewing their performance data, it was apparent that they were inconsistent in prospecting, which, in turn, was causing inconsistent results. They had adopted what I call a "double-down pattern." They would not generate the needed number of contacts this week but would plan to double their activity the following week—which rarely happened. They needed to generate the required level of activity each week. The solution was to meet weekly to review performance against the prospecting measures.

It was clear that they were very effective in closing business when they had an appointment. All I really needed to do was to hold them accountable for both getting the targeted number of referrals and calling referrals until they had made the targeted number of appointments. Granted, we had to work on resistance because none of them liked to prospect. We did things like breaking it down into short calling sessions rather than long calling sessions. But in the final analysis, they developed better prospecting habits because I would consistently remind them of the inevitable consequences: if you don't schedule appointments this week you won't have business next week. It's a case of nonnegotiable activities. As they consistently scheduled appointments their results improved impressively; all but one met or exceeded quota (the guy who didn't reach quota really resisted prospecting and stayed in the double-down pattern). One of the agents who became a company top performer started calling me her "million dollar warden." What gets measured gets done.

Let's apply the process to another example. A construction services company worked through the three-step job description process as part of a strategic planning initiative. The senior team, which included the production managers from the company's four production offices, focused on defining a superintendent's job. The team first defined outcomes for the job—what success looks like. They wanted superintendents to ensure that jobs were completed on time with as few mistakes as possible. What were the nonnegotiable activities that would drive successful outcomes for superintendents? As the team tackled that question it became clear to them that the best-performing superintendents walked their jobs every day, created a punch list (a record of incomplete or unsatisfactory construction items) for the job and were completely organized before the kickoff meeting each morning with their people and subs. They determined that these were nonnegotiable activities.

The team then addressed measurement. For instance, they created a "punch tracker" methodology to measure the punch list activity. The production managers made an interesting discovery once they started getting data from their newly instituted punch tracker methodology. They discovered that some of the superintendents that they had thought were doing a good job before they started measuring the activity were actually not doing as well as they thought. Others were actually doing a better job than they thought. By measuring the activity the company began to get consistently good performance on the key activity within about a month of implementation of measurement.

It is important to remember that a strategic job description is not static. The construction services company, for instance, added a key activity to the job description several months after first creating it. The company realized that the production managers were tracking completed punch lists but were not tracking completion of the items identified on the punch list. Another nonnegotiable activity was added to the job description. The production managers then turned to the superintendents to determine how to measure the activity. The superintendents came up with a very efficient way to measure the activity using technology. What really impressed me about the company's approach was that they got the people doing the work involved in creating the measurement. Not only were they able to identify an efficient measurement approach by getting the superintendents involved, they created ownership by the people doing the job.

The roll-out of the punch tracking methodology by Ben, one of the company's production managers, offers a great example of motivational competency. As we will explore in Part 2 of the book, the ability to strike a good balance between being serious and having fun is a highly motivational management practice. Ben gets it. He entered each one of his superintendents in a NASCAR (National Association for Stock Car Auto Racing) race for punch list results. He would post the punch standings in an e-mail written like he was calling a NASCAR race: "Coming up on the halfway point of the race, Andy—driving the black Corvette—is leading the tightly packed field but Earl appears to have missed a shift coming out of turn 2 dropping back a few spots. . . " The winner of the race received a gift certificate for a dinner. Ben was serious about getting the outcomes he wanted, but found a fun way to do it.

Whose Job Is It to Define the Job Description?

Creating a good job description—one that captures outcomes, nonnegotiable activities and measures—is the first step in getting the People Equation right. You are not merely describing a job; you are defining the success formula for the job. But whose job is it to define job descriptions?

The senior team and management of a company need to get involved because creating job descriptions is a strategic planning activity. They are the people who are ultimately responsible for the outcomes. I also understand that it is not practical for an executive to get involved in every job description. That being the case, I encourage the senior team and management to be hands-on regarding mission critical jobs.

Mission critical jobs are those jobs that are critically important in executing your business strategy. Generally about 20 percent of a company's jobs are mission critical. In their *Harvard Business Review* article, Mark Huselid, Richard Beatty and Brian Becker call these positions "A" positions. They explain that: "A single-minded focus on finding and delivering A players misses the point. A better approach is first to identify strategically critical jobs, then to invest disproportionately to ensure that the right people—doing the right things—are in those jobs."[8]

They also observe that very few companies systematically identify their strategically important "A" positions.[9] That's also been my experience.

It is important to note that "A" positions are not necessarily the highest level jobs; they are the highest impact jobs. FedEx offers a good example. A study asked human resource and business leaders to identify the key positions at Federal Express Asia Pacific. They named pilots, logistics designers, and top leaders. Certainly those are important positions. But the study found that couriers and dispatchers—comparatively undervalued positions—offered some of the largest opportunities to improve on-time performance and customer satisfaction.[10] It makes sense when you think about it. The couriers have high impact because they have direct contact with the customer; how they respond to customers can have an effect on efficiency and customer satisfaction. The couriers and dispatchers, for instance, make decisions on how to reconfigure a route and how long to wait for a customer's package. The study found that improving the quality of the courier-dispatcher talent pool had more impact potential than even improving pilot quality.[11] As with FedEx, you may find that some of your "A" positions are currently unrecognized or undervalued.

What are your "A" positions? One way to evaluate a position is to look at consequences. Look, for instance, at the consequences of a mistake. Ask yourself, "What are the consequences on customer satisfaction, efficiency, liability and/or profit of a mistake made by someone in that position?" If a mistake has a significant consequence, it's an "A" position. You can also look at the consequences of a wrong hire on customer satisfaction, efficiency and/or profit. A sales position, for instance, is almost always an "A" position because you risk lost sales opportunities by making a bad hire. The path to profitability is through the customer. Consider any position that can have a negative impact on customer service to be an "A" position. Look at your positions that have direct customer contact when defining "A" positions.

A company that sells technology products had to grapple with the consequences of mistakes that were being made by customer service reps; an "A" position for the company. Understanding a nonnegotiable activity was the key to correcting the mistakes. Here's what happened.

The customer service reps were the first point of customer contact. They were expected to provide fast and accurate processing of orders and coordinate with other departments to handle inquiries regarding pricing and billing and to coordinate with technicians to solve problems. Supervisors for the customer service department were getting a lot of calls from customers who were unhappy because they had been routed to the wrong technical resource. The problem was becoming chronic enough that senior management was getting involved. One of the managers asked what seemed to him to be a fairly obvious question, "Don't we train our reps in how to evaluate what kind of technical problem the customer has?" Long pause. "No. Not formally." Guess what happened when they started training customer services reps on how to assess a customer's technical problem? You guessed it, routing mistakes decreased.

You might be thinking that this situation was a blinding flash of the obvious. It was. But it is a very common occurrence. You can probably find instances of it in your organization right now. To ensure success we have to focus not only on the right people but also on ensuring that people are doing the right things—and have the training necessary to do the right things well. In this instance, evaluating the nature of a technical problem was a nonnegotiable activity: you couldn't be an effective rep if you didn't know how to route a customer. It was an activity that was easy to measure and easy to train. It was also an "A" position because making mistakes had a negative impact on customer satisfaction.

Why had they missed the obvious need for training? Because they had not consciously focused on or measured the activities that would drive outstanding customer service. That changed when senior management finally got involved. Senior management's response was reactive. I encourage management to be proactive by getting involved in creating strategic job descriptions—defining outcomes, nonnegotiable activities and measures—for "A" positions.

This company's experience shows that good things happen when leaders get deeply engaged in defining nonnegotiable activities—the things that must be done to succeed in a job. In the final analysis, a good business strategy will fall short of its goals if the activities required to execute it are not performed and performed well. In view of that consequence, getting involved in defining nonnegotiable activities is a strategic imperative.

A Simple Process for Determining the Numerator of the People Equation

The People Equation will help you apply the same degree of logic, rigor and strategic insight to hiring decisions that you would apply to other business decisions. An important part of that rigor is a focus on job activities. To do that you need a clear and repeatable analytical framework for analyzing job activities. That's the only way that you can get consistent results over time and determine the numerator of the People Equation. The following summarizes the process:

1. Identify your "A" positions.

2. Craft a job description for each of your "A" positions that sets out:
   - *Outcomes:* The outcomes you want—what

success looks like in the job.

- *Activities:* The key job activities that will drive those outcomes—the nonnegotiable things a person must do in order to succeed.
- *Measures.* The measures you will use to measure performance.

3. Craft job descriptions for remaining jobs using the same outcomes, activities and measures criteria.

The Appendix contains a simple worksheet that walks through outcomes, activities and measures. Although it is clearly not rocket science, I'm providing it because it has been a helpful template for clients as they have worked to describe their mission critical jobs.

When I work this worksheet I usually find that there are between four and seven nonnegotiable activities in a job. For instance, the Appendix also contains a job description created by the General Manager of manufacturing company for an "Operations Manager" position. He identifies five nonnegotiable activities in Section 5.0 of the job description. The first activity identified is: "Provide a safe and healthy manufacturing environment." There are certainly a lot of activities that go into providing a safe and healthy manufacturing environment. Another way to state the activity would be: "Take the steps needed to provide a safe and healthy manufacturing environment." The company has listed those steps in a procedural manual. Those steps or activities are actually in service of the broader activity of providing a safe and healthy manufacturing environment; you might think of them as supporting activities. If you end up with more than seven job activities, check to see if some of the activities are supporting activities.

The job description in the Appendix captures measurements in a separate section, number 6.0. The company's approach is to list both "lagging" and "leading" indicators. The first lagging indicator is: "RIR and Incident Severity meet annual targets." You obviously won't know if you have met your annual targets until the end of the year. To avoid surprise, the leading indicator measures a current activity. In this case the current activity for the company is: "Near miss reporting and safety training meets objectives." If your near miss reporting and safety training are meeting objectives, then you are on track to meet your annual target. If not, you can take the timely corrective action needed to achieve the annual target outcome you want.

Clearly defining the key elements of success—outcomes, nonnegotiable activities and performance measures—will not only help you get the People Equation right, it will ensure that you have clearly communicated performance expectations to each person in the company. You remove guessing and excuses: "But I thought I was supposed to do this. I didn't understand that is what you wanted." Clear communication is essential. As you will see in Part 2 of the book, good communication is one of the management practices that create motivational competency in a leader.

The numerator of the People Equation is about the right job; the denominator is about the right person. Once you have determined what the job requires, you are ready to get the right person for that job—the person with the right eligibility and suitability to perform the nonnegotiable activities of the job. Now let's take a look at the denominator.

People Equation Denominator: Eligibility

Right Education, Skills and Experience

$$\frac{\text{Key Job Activities}}{(\text{Eligibility} + \text{Suitability})} = \text{High Performance Potential}$$

A PERSON IS "ELIGIBLE" for a job if the person has the education, training and prior experience required to do the job activities. A resume primarily addresses a person's eligibility. It's fairly easy from a resume and interview to determine that a person has the level of education, skill and experience you're seeking. As I have indicated, the denominator of the People Equation includes both eligibility and suitability. In order to get the People Equation right you have to strike the right balance between eligibility and suitability: how much weight should you give to eligibility factors versus suitability factors? Let's first take a look at doctors, salespeople and lawyers to see what the right balance between eligibility and suitability looks like. Then I'll offer an analytical framework to help you strike the right balance between eligibility and suitability.

What Does the Right Balance Look Like?

Let's put eligibility and suitability on a scale in order to visualize the right balance for doctors, salespeople and lawyers. Imagine a large brass scale sitting on a desk. One side of the scale is eligibility and the other side is suitability. As you will see from the following examples, the scale for doctors is heavily tipped toward eligibility. For product sales and customer services positions, the scale is heavily tipped toward suitability. For sales of services the scale is going to be more balanced. If you are selling a technical service, like a legal service, there is going to be more weight on the eligibility side but a good amount of weight on suitability. When selling a service that is not technical, you may have more weight on the suitability side but a good amount of weight on the eligibility side. Let's discuss these weightings in more detail.

The scale is weighted heavily on the side of eligibility factors when it comes to doctors because education, skill and experience are obviously critically important when selecting a doctor. Do suitability factors carry any weight at all? The Vanderbilt University Medical Center says "yes." Good suitability in regard to a doctor is generally referred to as a good bedside manner—sensitivity to the patient as well as the patient's medical problem. Research from the Vanderbilt University Medical Center shows that doctors with lax bedside manners tend to get sued more often. Dr. Gerald Hickson, who has been a part of much of the Vanderbilt research, observed, "What sends people to lawyers are perceptions, not necessarily medical facts."[12] While this shows the importance of suitability, most people would and should still give more weight to education, skill and experience in selecting a doctor. The right balance looks like this: a heavy emphasis on eligibility and enough of a bedside manner to demonstrate sensitivity to the patient. Doctors—and their employers—are at risk if they assume education, skill and experience compensate for insensitivity.

The balance in sales tips the other way. Suitability factors are indispensable for consistent success in sales—factors such as the natural ability to communicate, build rapport and influence. Because suitability factors play such a key part in selling, it is widely held that you can select a sales-person for suitability alone and train for eligibility. I believe that there is a lot of truth in that—as long as you really do deliver on training. But it also depends on what you are selling. When you are selling services the scale needs to be more balanced: to succeed you may need more eligibility than you would need if you were selling a product. Let me explain.

Regardless of whether you are selling a product or service, you need to be able to build rapport, communicate effectively, be comfortable responding to objections and be influential; all suitability traits. You generally don't need a lot of eligibility when you sell a product. When you sell a product you are selling something that buyers can actually see and touch for themselves. Most suitable salespeople can fairly quickly learn the features and benefits they need to point out as well as the appropriate answers to a buyer's questions; on the other hand, you can't really teach suitability. Hence the conventional wisdom that you can select for suitability and train for eligibility.

By contrast, when you sell a service you are selling something that does not exist when you buy it; it's a promise to do something. As Harry Beckwith, best selling author of *Selling the Invisible*, points out, "You cannot hear the hum of a tax return being prepared, smell a good divorce attorney, or try on a dry cleaner to see if it flatters you. In most cases, you buy a service touch, taste, feel, smell, and sight unseen."[13] The knowledge and personal credibility of the salesperson becomes more important when you are selling something that is invisible. The more technical the service, the more knowledge and personal credibility the salesperson needs. The more technical the service, the more weight you are going to put on the eligibility side of the scale. Would you want to buy legal services from a salesperson for a law firm rather than a lawyer with the firm? You might be concerned whether the salesperson had enough legal expertise to really understand your problem. That's why law firms rarely have a sales force. When you are selling a service you need the level of eligibility necessary to build trust in a customer or client. That often takes some real subject matter expertise.

Striking the right balance between eligibility and suitability in sales was at the root of a lot of frustration Jeff, the CEO of a mid-market technology-related services company, was feeling. He was frustrated with his sales force. He had just gotten an e-mail from one of his salespeople asking him if he was available to help close a sale. "The salespeople always seem to need to get me or the VP of Sales involved to close a sale." There really was no big surprise there. The salespeople—or at least most of them—were good at opening a door and building rapport; they had enough subject matter knowledge to qualify an opportunity. And they could close the garden variety sales opportunities. The bigger opportunities had more complexity. Most of the salespeople did not have enough subject matter knowledge to effectively field a lot of the questions posed by buyers in these larger, more complex deals. Who did have the knowledge to close a sale? Jeff and VP of Sales. It was an eligibility issue. As he thought about it, Jeff realized that he did have the subject matter expertise to close the sale and that it was probably unrealistic to expect the salespeople to have his level of experience and knowledge. The same was true for the VP of Sales who had actually come up in the organization through operations. As Jeff let go of his frustration, he also realized that it actually reflected well on the salespeople that they knew that his involvement was a key to closing the bigger deal. He realized that he needed to think through the eligibility issue. As he did, he got a new view on how to build sales talent in the organization.

As Jeff thought through the eligibility issue he came up with a new game plan. He decided to play to the strengths of the current salespeople. He was not going to expect them to close the bigger deals without his support or support from the VP of Sales. He said, "Let's not throw out the baby with the bath water." That was important because, in his frustration, he wanted to replace the whole team. He still had to address the eligibility issue. He developed a training program to do that. He personally went through a Q & A exercise. Jeff framed the questions that he usually gets from prospective customers and then included the responses in the training manual. This approach to training has helped, but has not solved the problem. The current salespeople still need to team with Jeff or the VP of Sales to close the bigger sales. The long-term solution is to give greater weight to eligibility—certain types of subject matter knowledge and experience—when hiring salespeople.

Unfortunately, the company has not found many sales candidates that have the eligibility the company is seeking. So the company has developed an apprentice program to develop eligibility. The company is hiring people with good sales qualities and experience and requiring them to spend almost a year working in operations to ensure that they have the needed eligibility.

The teaming approach to sales—teaming a good salesperson with a subject matter expert—is a common approach used to strike the needed balance between sales suitability and eligibility. I call this team approach a "Batman and Robin" sales strategy. Here's why.

It has to do with the relationship of Martin and Robin. Martin sold technology products for years. He is an outstanding salesman. He knows everyone—he has an amazing Rolodex. When his company began to sell services as well as products, Martin realized that selling services was the wave of the future. Martin decided to move into the services space as he saw margins continue to compress on product sales. Martin realized that he needed more eligibility—subject matter expertise. The company had hired a sharp young engineer named Robin. Martin started taking Robin on sales calls. A classic partnership was born. They have sold a tremendous amount of business together earning them the moniker "the dynamic duo"—Batman and Robin. When thinking through eligibility issues in sales it is helpful to ask yourself if you need a dynamic duo. In the case of the VP of Sales mentioned earlier, the answer would be "no." He came up in operations and also has high sales suitability. He can do it himself. In regard to most of his salespeople, by contrast, the answer is "yes." For them he is part of a dynamic duo. To carry forward the visual of the scale, you need to determine if Batman has enough weight—experience and knowledge—to carry off the particular sale. If not, you need to add a little Robin to strike the appropriate balance.

In most cases—other than in sales or customer service types of positions—I find that companies tend to give undue weight to eligibility factors. That is certainly the case in law. Most law firms are misguided in their selection practices because they tend to consider eligibility factors related to education, skill and experience almost to the exclusion of other factors. Clearly those factors are the top priority. But law is also a business. The most successful lawyers tend to be both good practitioners and good at developing clients. That's the message William J. Flannery, Jr. champions. Flannery is a market leader in training his fellow lawyers to develop business. In his engaging book, *The Lawyer's Field Guide to Effective Business Development*, he debunks a number of myths about lawyers and business development. I particularly like Myth #6: "Lawyers who need to do business development are probably not good lawyers, and that is why they do not have a solid, big 'book of business.'"[14] In industry parlance, a "book of business" is a list of clients or accounts. Indeed, lawyers that do not have a solid book of business are probably not actively developing a book of business. I had the good fortune of practicing law during the gold rush days in the 1980s when there was more demand for lawyers than there was supply. That's not true today. Today business development is a nonnegotiable activity for most lawyers. To be successful today, lawyers need to have a good balance between their education and experience in law and the suitability traits that support success in business development. Unfortunately many talented lawyers relate to business development much like Vince Vaughn's character relates to washing dishes in the movie *The Break-up* discussed earlier: they try to avoid it. As Flannery points out, "It is not surprising that many lawyers, faced with the necessity of building business, often find it an onerous task or even try to evade it insofar as possible. People are rarely comfortable attempting complex tasks for which they feel unprepared, especially tasks that depend on their personal qualities."[15] Chris is an example.

Chris is a lawyer in a large and well-regarded law firm. Very bright guy. He was Order of the Coif in law school— that's like Phi Beta Kappa for lawyers. I was having lunch with Chris a few years ago and he was bemoaning the rapid ascendency in the firm of one of our contemporaries, Shawn. Shawn had joined the firm after being referred by one of the firm's clients; Chris had been hotly recruited out of law school for his high grades. Shawn was a good lawyer but, Chris was right, not nearly as good a lawyer as Chris. But Shawn had gained a higher stature in the firm and was making a lot more money than Chris. Why? Two words: business development. Shawn has great rapport traits and has developed an impressive list of clients over the years. The firm was clearly not misguided in selecting Shawn. The firm selected a lawyer who had the right balance between eligibility and suitability to develop a strong practice. In an interesting turn of fate, most of Chris' work has ended up being for Shawn's clients. Chris is one of the lawyers that Flannery describes. He finds business development "onerous."

To pull these examples together, let's take a look at that large brass scale sitting on a desk. On one side of the scale is eligibility and on the other side is suitability. For doctors the scale is heavily tipped toward eligibility. For product sales and customer services positions, the scale is heavily tipped toward suitability. For sales of services the scale is going to be more balanced. If you are selling a technical service there is going to be more weight on the eligibility side but a good amount of weight on suitability. When selling a nontechnical service you may have more weight on the suitability side but still a good amount of weight on the eligibility side.

Analytical Framework:
How Do You Balance the Scale?

There is a simple analytical process that will help you strike the right balance between eligibility and suitability. It starts with the following two steps:

Step 1: Define the numerator for the People Equation: identify the nonnegotiable activities required for success in the job.

Step 2: For each nonnegotiable activity ask yourself how much education, training and experience is required to perform the activity well.

As an example, let's look at how these first two steps in the process helped achieve the right balance in a sales support position. A company had a history of performance problems and high turnover in the sales support position. As the job was described to me, it was clear that the company viewed the job as primarily a customer service position. That surprised me because, in my experience, it is generally an administrative job. I asked them to identify the nonnegotiable job activities. They were surprised that their final list included mostly administrative activities like entering data and tracking orders. In reality the position did not really require that much customer contact. They got it. They needed to put more weight on the skill and experience needed to be good at the administrative activities they had identified. They also needed to rethink the suitability component of the job. They needed to factor in the Enjoyment Performance Theory criteria.

Enjoyment Performance Theory explains that the person best suited for the sales support position would be a person who:

1. Enjoys the tasks required by that job.
2. Has interests that relate to the job.
3. Likes the work environment and the interpersonal interactions involved in and required by the job.

People who gravitate toward customer service jobs tend to enjoy tasks related to people rather than tasks related to entering and tracking data. They had not only been overlooking important eligibility factors for the job, they were hiring based on the wrong suitability criteria: they were hiring people in sales support who liked working with people rather than people who enjoyed administrative activities. No wonder they experienced a lot of turnover.

The hiring managers' perspectives on the sales support position were unusual. They had not put enough weight on eligibility factors. Again, in most cases, I find companies put too much emphasis on eligibility factors. Why do people tend to overemphasize eligibility factors? I think it's generally because they don't have a good analytical framework with which to evaluate suitability factors. That's certainly where I started when I began to work out the People Equation. The next section of the book is designed to give you a solid analytical framework to assess suitability factors. As the example of the sales support position illustrates, both eligibility and suitability are important. Striking a good balance between eligibility and suitability begins with understanding the nonnegotiable activities in the job, the numerator of the People Equation, and then asking questions about both eligibility and suitability. To do that, the following steps 3 and 4 are added to the first two steps:

Step 1: Define the numerator for the People Equation: identify the nonnegotiable activities required for success in the job.

Step 2: For each nonnegotiable activity ask yourself how much education, training and experience is required to perform the activity well.

Step 3: For each nonnegotiable activity ask yourself what kind of suitability is required to perform the activity well. The following section in the book will help you answer this question.

Step 4: Based on your answers to the questions in steps 2 and 3, strike the balance. For example, if most of the activities require a heavy dose of education and experience, then the scale will be weighted more heavily toward eligibility.

Before we leave this section I would like to add a couple of insights on eligibility factors themselves. It is helpful to consider both optimum levels of eligibility as well as priority of eligibility factors.

Eligibility factors are typically identified in terms of minimum requirements—must haves. For instance, a candidate must have a minimum level of education, a minimum number of years in a similar job and/or a minimum level of proficiency in using a software program. Companies often stop there. You will get a clearer picture of eligibility if you look at both "needed" eligibility and "optimum" eligibility—must have and want to have. If you require two years as the minimum level of experience in a similar job, what is the optimum level of experience you would want? Two years is enough, but five years really would be better.

In section 4.0 of the job description in the Appendix, the company lists "preferred" or "optimum" eligibility requirements for education, licensing and experience. The company may not always be able to find a candidate with optimum eligibility, or may not have the budget to hire someone with optimum eligibility. Still, going through the process of defining optimum eligibility is important. Thinking through the level of education, training, skill and experience that will best promote success in the job, gives you the most complete insight into eligibility. It may also open your mind to possibilities. Think back to the services company discussed in this section. Not finding salespeople with the desired eligibility prompted the company to supplement its training manual and start an apprentice program. Knowing the level of education and skill that best promotes success in the job may prompt employees to seek that education and skill independently. Being clear about the level of eligibility you want increases your chance of getting it.

It's also helpful to rank eligibility factors. Are certain factors more important than other factors? If proficiency in using a software program, for instance, is more important to you than the years of prior work experience, you would give that eligibility factor more weight or priority in your hiring decision. Your highest priority eligibility factors should naturally correspond to nonnegotiable activities. Rethink the priority if they don't align. In the sales support position we discussed, for instance, proficiency in using your tracking system should probably be a high priority eligibility factor if you list ability to track orders as a nonnegotiable activity. If it's not, you might want to rethink your priorities.

People Equation Denominator: Suitability

Right Person

$$\frac{\text{Key Job Activities}}{(\text{Eligibility} + \text{Suitability})} = \text{High Performance Potential}$$

WHAT DO WARREN BUFFET and Sun Tzu, the Chinese general who wrote *The Art of War* in the 6th Century BC, have to do with getting the right person in a job? As you will see in this section of the book, they both give helpful insights into understanding a person's suitability for a job. My biggest epiphany in understanding how to get the People Equation right is that "suitability" is a defining quality of an "A" player. You certainly have to know that the candidate can do the job—has the education and experience needed to do the job. But "A" players not only can do the job, they also want to do the job and have the situational awareness to do the job well. This section of the book will paint a more complete picture of how these suitability factors define a top performer—an "A" player.

A fundamental difference between hiring decisions and decisions about financial capital, products, services, customers and technology is that we generally lack reliable data when making hiring decisions. The only data we generally have access to in making a hiring decision is a resume and the information we glean from an interview and references. It's difficult to reliably assess suitability from an interview, resume or reference. That does not mean that the interview is not an important part of the selection process. But to infuse people decisions with logic and rigor you need reliable data. Fortunately, advancements in job assessment technology can now provide you with reliable data. Suitability factors are hard to pin down because they are intangible; job assessment technology can now make them tangible. That's really great news for the people in the trenches. One of the most exciting things I can share with you in this book is how breakthroughs in assessment technology can now give you reliable data on these intangibles—make the elusive concrete for you. As we explore the dynamics of suitability in this section of the book we will take a look at both the objective data provided by assessment technology as well as how to maximize the more subjective information you get from an interview.

Bottom line: to make suitability practical, two questions need to be answered. What is job suitability? How do we apply today's technology to assess it?

What is Job Suitability?

Enjoyment is a fundamental behavioral principle in understanding suitability: we tend to do the things we like to do and avoid—as much as possible—the things we don't like to do. People who are well-suited for a job enjoy the activities required by the job. Dr. Harrison's research demonstrates that employees who enjoy at least 75 percent of their job activities are three times more likely to succeed than employees who enjoy less than 75 percent of their job.[16] You may, however, enjoy the activities in a job but not have the situational awareness to do the job well. Again, although the term "situational awareness" can reference a field of study, I am simply using the term to mean how an individual manages his relationship with himself and with others. Let's take a look in more detail at how enjoyment and situational awareness fuse to make someone well-suited for a job.

The "Joy Factor"

Billionaire Warren Buffet told a group of students at the University of Nebraska: "I may have more money than you, but money doesn't make the difference. . . If there is any difference between you and me, it may simply be that I get up every day and have a chance to do what I love to do, every day. If you want to learn anything from me, this is the best advice I can give you."[17] Although there are obviously other differences, it is interesting that Warren Buffet believes that enjoying what he does makes the most important difference. His conclusion is consistent with Dr. Harrison's research. Buffet clearly has what I call the "joy factor."

The joy factor is simply cause and effect. Enjoyment Performance Theory explains that enjoying an activity causes us to do it more often; the effect is that we get better because we tend to get better at an activity as we do it more. Getting better, in turn, reinforces our enjoyment of the activity. In sports vernacular we would be talking about "reps." A comment I ran across in a sports column recently says it well. Greg Alexander, a University of Hawaii junior football quarterback, commented, "The more reps [repetitions] you get, the more you can get into a rhythm and the more you get a feel for everything that is going on . . . So obviously the more you play the better you feel you get."[18] On the other hand if we don't like doing something we tend to do it less often with the effect of not getting better.

The important dynamic at play is that as human beings we tend to engage when we like doing something and resist when we don't like doing something. In any job there may be some activities that we resist doing. You know those types of activities. They're the ones we put off until the eleventh hour or the ones we muster up the resolve to get done—put our nose to the grind stone and grind it out. We will tend to perform better in a job if the majority of activities—at least 75 percent— are activities we enjoy, rather than activities we grind out. By way of example, let me share my own experience.

I spent the first decade of my career as a corporate lawyer; most of that time with a large law firm. The majority of my job activities required a great deal of attention to detail. Enjoyment Performance Theory would suggest that if I tended to enjoy tasks that require a great deal of attention to detail, I would do them more often and develop a high attention to detail and patience. Frankly, I don't particularly enjoy activities that require a great attention to detail; but I have a very high achievement drive. I did the work out of resolve—nose-to-the-grindstone—rather than out of enjoyment. I still developed my ability because I was spending a lot of time involved in the activities. I had good eligibility and the more time I spent practicing law, the better I performed. Although I was successful, I didn't wake up every day and do something I loved like Warren Buffet. I had the privilege, however, to work with several attorneys who were passionate about law. One day I was involved in a conversation about a transaction with two of these outstanding lawyers who were senior partners with the firm. They got into a lengthy debate about a minute point of law. As I listened to them it struck me that they *relished* the conversation. I was taking part in the conversation out of a commitment to deliver good results; they were totally engaged.

Think for a moment about job activities in which you get naturally engaged. You probably don't associate words like "toil," "labor," "stress" or "effort" with those activities. They may even energize you. By contrast, think about activities that you don't like doing, but nonetheless put your nose to the grindstone and grind them out. You probably do associate words like "toil," "stress" and "effort" with those activities. We all have to do some of those activities. The important point is that the majority of the activities in our jobs should not be nose-to-the-grindstone activities. Nose-to-the-grindstone performance is generally not sustainable over long periods of time regardless of capability and determination; it takes too much energy. We have to manage too much internal resistance.

I discovered that I really enjoy business, and I now get deeply engaged with what I do. I have the joy factor that was missing when I practiced law. I have found that job satisfaction is exponential when I align my achievement drive with truly enjoying what I'm doing.

I was riding my bike one morning after writing about my law firm experience. I turned into some wind as I rode the bike up a hill—well, as much of a hill as we have in Louisiana. As I felt the resistance, I thought that my experience practicing law was a lot like what I was experiencing on the bike. The difference was that my resistance was internal. Handling that internal resistance took as much energy as it took to manage the external forces of resistance I faced on the bike. Frankly, I like it much better going downhill with the wind at my back. Certainly in life—and any job—we are going to experience some wind and some hills. But when joy envelops the parts we resist, we have a very different experience. Work becomes more like riding with the wind at our backs. The passionate lawyers I mentioned seemed to enjoy the ride that I pushed through. Although we were doing the same activities, they did them with the wind at their back and I did them pushing through internal resistance.

It's understandable why Herb Kelleher first looked for good attitude. Low resistance to job activities is a dependable indicator of a good attitude. That's why applying Enjoyment Performance Theory is so effective in assessing job suitability.

One of the most rewarding things for me in my career has been helping clients with whom I consult ingrain the joy factor in their companies by hiring and promoting based on suitability as well as eligibility. I have worked with the concept since 2002; through experience, it has morphed into the more complete People Equation.

To factor joy into the People Equation requires two steps:

1. You first have to identify what a person naturally likes to do; the person's natural interests, qualities and traits. For instance: the person is naturally attentive to detail and enjoys detailed tasks; the person naturally gravitates to planning and likes planning activities; the person has qualities such as warmth, empathy and tact that give rise to natural rapport and effectiveness in managing conflict.

2. You can then align the traits, qualities and interests to the activities you want performed. This, of course, requires you to define the numerator of the People Equation. For instance, if the activities you have defined require attention to detail and planning, the person who is naturally attentive to detail and likes planning activities would be most suitable for your job.

Obviously, the challenge is in identifying a person's natural traits and qualities. That's where current assessment technology is invaluable. Before we take an in-depth look at assessment technology, let's consider the impact of situational awareness on job suitability.

Situational Awareness

Knowing how to manage yourself and your relationships with others is essential if you are going to be well-suited for a job. There is a passage from Sun Tzu's *The Art of War* that gives perspective into situational awareness:

> "So it is said that if you know others and know yourself, you will not be imperiled in a hundred battles; if you do not know others but know yourself, you win one and lose one; if you do not know others and do not know yourself, you will be imperiled in every single battle."[20]

Poor situational awareness is at the root of much of the litany of counter-productive behaviors that create discord and disagreement in companies—behaviors that are controlling, defensive, critical, dogmatic, permissive, harsh, dominating, inflexible or insensitive to name a few. These are counter-productive behaviors that can derail a promising career.

In their landmark study on executive derailment for the Center for Creative Leadership, Jean Brittain Leslie and Ellen Van Velsor looked at why executives that had been identified as having high potential early in their careers, had a string of successes and were seen as "technical geniuses or tenacious problem-solvers," had, nonetheless, derailed as they moved up in the organization. The two most common reasons cited were:

- "Poor working relationships"—alienating those they worked with by being too harsh, critical, demanding or insensitive.

- "Inability to develop and adapt"—not open to feedback, being "pig-headed," not learning from mistakes and not pursuing self-development.[21]

In short, what I call a lack of situational awareness. As the study says: "Problems with Interpersonal Relationships is the theme that more than any other, reveals the negative aspects of character that derail managers . . . In the research, managers who are seen as having problems with interpersonal relationships are described as insensitive, manipulative, critical, demanding, authoritarian, self-isolating, or aloof."[22]

It's like a great basketball player that has the talent and love of the game but plays for individual glory at the expense of teamwork. Players like that miss what legendary UCLA basketball coach John Wooden said is the key to stardom: "The main ingredient of stardom is the rest of the team."[23]

The interesting thing is that the problem with interpersonal relationships is often the result of *too much of a good thing*. The executive derailment study found that while "ambition or being ambitious" is viewed as a success factor, that being "too ambitious" can be a derailment factor.[24] Jim Collins reached a similar conclusion in his book *Good to Great*. He observes that during pivotal transition years every one of the good-to-great companies he studied had what he calls "Level 5" leadership (the highest level in a hierarchy of executive capabilities). He writes, "Level 5 leaders embody a paradoxical mix of personal humility and professional will. They are ambitious, to be sure, but ambition first and foremost for the company, not themselves."[25] Consistent with the derailment study research, Collins notes the irony that the personal ambition that often drives people to positions of power can stand at odds with what is required for Level 5 leadership.[26]

The concept that effectiveness is the result of a "paradoxical mix" of traits is a very important concept in getting the People Equation right. Collins found, for instance, that Level 5 leaders were "a study in duality: modest and willful, humble and fearless."[27] We all possess and demonstrate these seemingly contradictory traits simultaneously. And that's a good thing. The paradox is that effectiveness is the result of a good blending of these seemingly contradictory traits. A problem develops when you don't have a good blending; you have too much of one trait and not enough of the other. Let's revisit the earlier discussion of communication as an example.

When we communicate we all—to a lesser or greater extent—possess the qualities of directness and tact. Directness and tact both contribute to effective communication even though they seem to be opposite or contradictory. To be an effective communicator you need to be able to communicate frankly or tactfully as the situation requires. If you tend to be more direct than tactful and you encounter a situation that requires tact, you may communicate poorly by being too direct for the situation. Your bluntness may be perceived as rudeness. You are not responding effectively to the situation because you have too much of a good thing: too much directness.

Remember Eric, the IT hire? His lack of situational awareness was the root of his failure at the IT company discussed in the opening pages of this book. Although Eric's job required him to be authoritative in order to succeed, he also needed to enroll his people in the decision rather than merely direct them. Therein is the paradox; one that he did not execute well. By not including his people he alienated them and diminished his influence, his authority and ultimately his success. He lacked suitability because he was authoritarian rather than managing with a good balance of authority and inclusion. It turns out it was a classic example of the derailing behaviors identified in the derailment study.

Although I know in hindsight that a lack of situational awareness was a problem in regard to Eric, that does not solve the problem. We needed to know that he lacked situational awareness "before" we hired him. I imagine that at this point you might be thinking to yourself, "Great. I'm not a psychologist; I'm just trying to make a hiring decision. How am I going to assess whether a candidate has the right *paradoxical mix* of traits before I hire him? Get real." Relax... advances in assessment technology can give you that data. Let's take a look at how assessment technology can give you the data you need on a person's natural traits and qualities as well as insight into a person's situational awareness—before you hire the person.

How Do You <u>Assess</u> Job Suitability?

Being able to successfully assess job suitability is obviously where the rubber meets the road. You need good data. Telling you that the joy factor together with paradoxical pairs of traits need to be considered in making a good hiring decision without telling you how to assess them falls short—you don't have a usable analytical framework. Let me first show you how today's technology can give you reliable data and then show you how to make the information you glean from an interview more useful.

Assessment Technology

Thanks to today's technology, businesspeople have access to job-matching tools that provide reliable, in-depth insights into an individual's basic strengths, weaknesses and motivations as they relate to a specific job. In short, reliable data. The key to achieving reliable data is to ensure that you are using an assessment tool that produces results that correlate to a specific job.

There are literally hundreds of assessment tools on the market. But the vast majority of assessments were not developed for the workplace with the goal of predicting actual job performance. Personality assessments have been around for about 60 years. They are not, however, job-behavior assessments and their validation is not relevant to job performance. You can be frustrated with the results if you are looking for objective job-related data and all you get is insight into a person's personality. To get the People Equation right you need a good job-matching tool. Using the right tool has made a profound difference in my and my clients' ability to make good hiring and promoting decisions. How do you identify a good job-matching tool? The following questions provide criteria to help you identify a job-matching tool that will give you the usable data input you need for making talent decisions:

1. Is the assessment job-related?

2. Is the assessment based on job performance research? An assessment is reliable if the author of the assessment can demonstrate that it was based on having assessed the actual performance of a broad number of people over multiple years. It is important to note that a valid assessment does not discriminate against individuals based on age, sex, race, natural origin or religion.

3. Assessments are based on questionnaires. Is the questionnaire easy to administer? With today's technology, it should be web-based.

4. Are the results easy to understand? In making a business decision—whether the decision is a financial or hiring decision—data alone is not enough. It has to be accessible to the person making the business decision. I have read some assessment reports that are so complex and full of jargon that they require a skilled professional to decipher the bottom line. Look for

instruments that include clear, simple narratives on the person's strengths, weaknesses and motivations.

An assessment tool that satisfies these criteria can provide objective data that is vital to making a good business decision regarding hiring and promoting.

It is also helpful to consider the number of traits the assessment tool defines. A large number of traits gives you the ability to infuse nuance—subtle differences—into your talent decision. As you evaluate job-matching tools, you will find some tools measure 10 to 30 traits and others measure over 100. It's like the difference between the 8-pack and the 96-pack of Crayola Crayons.

When I married my wife, who is an interior designer and great colorist, my color sense was fairly well contained within the 8-pack of Crayons. I had the basic colors down: red, yellow, green, blue, black, brown, orange and purple. My wife, however, played with the jumbo 96-pack. She could see nuances of color that I didn't even know existed. Who knew that grey could have green undertones? But over the years she has expanded my range of colors. I can now see nuances of color. I can now also see nuances in a person's performance traits because I have worked with an assessment instrument, the Harrison Assessment™, which looks at more than 100 traits. I encourage you to go for the jumbo 96-pack when selecting an assessment tool—it will help you develop your ability to see nuances in performance.

There are a number of good job-matching assessments on the market. With the numerous references I have made to Dr. Harrison's work, it's probably no surprise that my assessment tool of choice for my clients is the assessment tool he developed. Since I first began using the Harrison Assessment in 2002, it has been highly predictive of job success and has given my clients clear and objective data on job suitability. To be candid, my clients and I are continually amazed at the penetrating insights we are able to glean from the data. I want to be forthright with you as a reader regarding my strong bias in favor of the Harrison Assessment. My bias is so strong that I am a distributor of the assessment. Regardless of my personal bias, however, I encourage each company to use diligence to find the assessment tool that best suits its strategic objectives and culture. That's why I have provided you with guidelines for selecting an assessment. Remember also that the People Equation is more than an assessment tool. It is a proactive process to reduce the risk of a bad hire; it incorporates assessment data as a part of the process.

Like all reliable assessment tools, the Harrison Assessment is job-related, based on 20 years of comprehensive job performance data, and is web based. It measures 156 traits—it's a "jumbo 156-pack" assessment. It can also be easily customized to identify the traits shared by the top performers in your particular job. It answers the question: what makes the top performers in your company perform better than everyone else? That's an important question.

You use an assessment tool to help you hire and develop your next high performer—someone who performs like your current high performers. What traits do your top performers share in common? That was a hard question to answer before job assessment technology developed to its present level of sophistication. What made top performers different was like a secret sauce: you might be able to identify some elements, but the combination remained largely a mystery.

It's like a client of mine who tried to replicate the secret sauce from a favorite New Orleans restaurant. He loved the barbecue shrimp at Pascal Manale's in New Orleans—the restaurant originated the dish and the sauce is exceptional! He tried to replicate the sauce at his home in Florida. He got close, but it was just never quite the same. One day he found the recipe posted on the internet. Once he saw the recipe he knew what ingredients he was missing. He now makes a mean barbecue shrimp! All he needed was some missing data.

Using assessment data, I have been able to help companies recognize the recipe for their "secret sauce": the traits and qualities that are shared by their top performers. Once you know the recipe, you can consistently select for those traits and qualities and hire and promote top performers.

The traits that define top performers often surprise me. For instance, Harrison Assessment research determined that the top performing salespeople at a national life insurance company had a very high natural desire to teach or instruct. Although I would not have expected that to be an ingredient in the secret sauce for insurance agents, once it was identified it made sense. Life insurance salespeople at that company spend the majority of their workday educating people on life insurance and other financial products. Because they enjoy educating, they naturally get very engaged in the process of explaining complicated insurance concepts. Their sales success reflects the joy factor at play. Natural desire to teach and educate is a trait that the company now looks for when hiring salespeople. It's an important part of their recipe for performance success—their secret sauce. It has also proven to be an ingredient in the secret sauce of several of my clients that sell products or services that require educating a buyer.

One not-so-secret ingredient in performance success is situational awareness. A person with good situational awareness is well-balanced in his relationship with others and with himself; as well as in his ability to exercise good judgment. We are most effective in a situation—have the needed situational awareness—when we are able to strike a good balance between paradoxical traits and thereby avoid the "too much of a good thing" problem the derailment study identified. The muscles in our bodies offer a good analogy.

The traits that create good situational awareness are like muscles in the body. Just like all bodies have muscles, we all have the traits that create good situational awareness. We all have the potential for good situational awareness. But you have to hone and balance the traits that produce good situational awareness just like you have to develop and tone your muscles to produce body strength.

Let's apply this muscle analogy to bluntness: being too frank for the situation. Think of the right arm muscle as frankness and the left arm muscle as tactfulness. Frankness and tactfulness both contribute to good situational awareness when you are communicating. If you have a lot of strength in your right arm (frankness) and very little strength in your left arm (tact), you will tend to rely on the right arm and be overly frank—blunt. To have good situational awareness, you need to have a good balance of strength in your left and right arms—a good balance of strength between frankness and tactfulness. That way, you can rely on the strength of the muscle that will make you most effective in the situation. It's like a friend of mine who took up boxing.

He tells me that although you use your right arm to throw the power punch—the right cross—you use your left arm 70 percent of the time throwing a left jab. You can't win a fight unless you have both a strong right cross and a strong left jab. He worked on developing both so that he would be able to respond to whatever was thrown at him in the ring.

When coaching people to develop better situational awareness, I encourage them to focus on developing the underdeveloped muscle. If you have a strong right cross, work on the left jab. By developing the underdeveloped muscle, you're able to flex the strength of the left arm or right arm as the situation requires.

Authoritative and collaborative are another pair of traits that combine to contribute to good situational awareness. Dr. Harrison refers to "authoritative" as a dynamic trait and "collaborative" as a gentle trait. You are most effective when you can strike a balance between the dynamic and gentle—you have both a strong right cross and left jab. "Authoritative" is defined as "the desire for decision-making authority and the willingness to accept decision-making authority." Certainly it is a trait needed for success in a decision-making role. "Collaborative" is defined as "the tendency to collaborate with others when making decisions." A person who has developed strength in both the authoritative and collaborative traits—has balance—is able to be authoritative or collaborative *as the situation requires.* That person has good situational awareness. On the other hand, a person who tends to be authoritative but not very collaborative will tend to be authoritarian. Authoritarian behavior is counter-productive because it is over-controlling, limits input of information and perspectives and tends to alienate others who have a stake in an outcome.

The principle is that you can prevent counter-productive behavior by developing strength in two traits that seem like opposites. The Harrison Assessment identifies 12 of these paradoxical pairs of traits in its proprietary application of Paradox Theory (Paradox Technology™). Some show how you manage your relationship with yourself, some show how you manage your relationship with others and some relate to how you make decisions. Frankness-and-tact and authoritative-and-collaborative are two of the twelve paradoxical pairs. The following summarizes some of the others. This summary will give you a perspective on what you need to look for when you make a talent decision so that you can identify the potential for derailing behavior.

Examples of paradoxical pairs of traits that impact how you manage your relationship with yourself:

ᐒ **Paradoxical pair: self-acceptance _and_ a commitment to improve.**

People with strong "self-acceptance" have a solid sense of their self-worth and a realistic view of their current capabilities. To have good situational awareness, self-acceptance needs to be balanced by a strong desire to improve, to expand current capabilities. Hiring people with a positive, but realistic, view of self diminishes defensiveness in an organization.

ᐒ **Paradoxical pair: a tendency to maintain order in an environment _and_ the ability to be flexible.**

Good balance between these two traits results in an ability to adapt to change. As the executive derailment study shows, the ability to adapt is critically important to success. I believe it becomes increasingly important as the rate of change continues to escalate. Too strong a tendency to maintain order results in rigidity and resistance to change.

Examples of paradoxical pairs of traits that impact how you manage your relationship with others:

- ❧ **Paradoxical pair: confidence in your own viewpoint <u>and</u> openness to exploring others' viewpoints.**

  Confidence becomes arrogance without this important balance. Balancing confidence with openness means that you are confident in your viewpoint on a matter but also interested in what I think about the matter. If you are open to what I think, I will naturally be more prone to listen to you. How many times have you heard someone say, "Bob and I have a great relationship because he is a great talker"? Or, "Jill and I have a great relationship because she is always right"?

- ❧ **Paradoxical pair: enforcing rules or giving direction <u>and</u> being sensitive to the impact of the rules or direction on individuals.**

  Rules and directives are a positive force for achieving accountability and general fairness in an organization. But how they are enforced has an impact on individual relationships. One of the true masters of this paradox is an owner of a very successful third-generation family-owned business. The company has phenomenally low turnover. I once asked him why he thought the turnover rate was so low. He quickly answered, "Because my father taught me to always say 'because.'" He went on to explain that his father taught him that people want to know why they are being asked to do something, so a good manager let's them know "why." As I've listened to him, he does consistently say "because." I have observed that he also tends to say, "I understand." For instance, I once heard him say to an administrator for the company, "I want you to do something that I understand is not your job and that will create additional work for you. I am asking you to do it because we don't have anyone else who has the knowledge on this kind of job that you do." Before he made the request he had obviously paused to consider the impact that his direction was going to have on the employee. He was able to communicate the directive in a way that was both empathetic and decisive. As I said, he's a master at the paradox. He has achieved balance. By contrast, a lack of balance in this paradox can result in harshness (strong on enforcing and weak on empathy) or permissiveness (strong on empathy and weak on enforcement).

Examples of paradoxical pairs of traits that impact good judgment:

   ଔ **Paradoxical pair: optimism <u>and</u> assessment of potential pitfalls.**

   Striking a good balance here shapes positive but realistic expectations. Too much optimism results in blind optimism; too little optimism results in skepticism.

   ଔ **Paradoxical pair: confidence in your own viewpoint <u>and</u> openness to exploring others' viewpoints.**

   This paradox not only positively impacts relationships; it also improves your exercise of good judgment. You will make better decisions if you are willing to adjust your perspective based on insights gained from others.

In order to get the People Equation right you have to know the traits that make someone suitable for the job, and you have to know that the person does not have too much of a trait. A manager needs to be authoritative but not authoritarian. A leader needs to be confident but not arrogant. Fortunately you can gain insight into whether a candidate has too much of a good thing—is prone to counter-productive behavior—with assessment technology. The bottom line is that technology based on in-depth, job-specific performance research can now make the current level of a person's situational awareness identifiable and quantifiable for anyone making a hiring decision.

Individuals who are not effective in managing their relationship with themselves and with others—individuals who lack situational awareness—are what Scott, the VP of Sales for a mid-market client of mine, calls "high maintenance employees." He has some high performance salespeople who are good at their jobs but who also create collateral damage in the organization through counter-productive behavior. He likes the Harrison Assessment paradox graphs because he can see if a job candidate is potentially high maintenance. With that data, he can make the business decision on whether he wants to take on the management challenge for himself and the organization. Sometimes he's willing to take on the challenge; sometimes he's not. What's important is that he is able to make an informed decision based on objective data provided by reliable assessment technology.

Having explored how to bring objectivity into a talent decision using assessment technology, we also need to consider the role subjectivity plays in a talent decision. Objectivity paired with the more subjective assessment gathered in an interview results in a balanced and comprehensive approach to a talent decision. Let's take a look at the interview.

The Interview

A good assessment process includes both subjective and objective assessment. The interview is, by definition, subjective. Despite its shortcomings and the availability of more objective means of selection, the interview, done properly, still provides important insights. One valuable contribution the interview makes is in determining whether you like the person. Whether you like someone is a matter of personal judgment and you can't get that from an instrument. Let's take a look at some of the benefits and risks of the interview along with some tips on how to get the most out of an interview.

"Fit" is a core concept in making a good talent decision. There are three components of fit to evaluate: fit with the job, fit with company and fit with a manager. Although a good assessment tool will give you concrete data on each component of fit, there is still an intangible: likability. The interview is necessary to assess likability.

The research about doctors discussed earlier show that doctors with a good bedside manner get sued less often. Likability is very potent. It is a key influence principle. Robert B. Cialdini, a leading authority on influence, states, "People prefer to say yes to individuals they know and like. Recognizing this rule, compliance professionals commonly increase their effectiveness by emphasizing several factors that increase their overall attractiveness and likability."[28] Bottom line: we tend to say "yes" to a candidate we like. Liking a person is an important dimension of fit. We are moving toward a good fit if we like a candidate and the candidate likes us. There is, however, a **very high risk** inherent in the natural process of determining likability.

There is an unconscious human tendency to make a snap judgment on likability. Therein lies the risk. Snap your fingers. No, go ahead; snap your fingers. Research shows that we form first impressions in the little amount of time as it takes for us to snap our fingers. And once we've made that snap first impression, it has a powerful influence on our final decision. First impressions tend to create a "halo effect."

The "halo effect" is a classic finding in social psychology. It was first identified in 1920 by Edward Thorndike, an American psychologist. The halo effect happens when one good aspect of a candidate (e.g., likability) makes the candidate look good in other areas as well. If your first impression is positive, then it's as if the candidate is surrounded by an angelic halo. We tend to attribute other positive traits to an individual we like, even though we have no specific information regarding that trait. We fall into like.

The reverse is true. A "horns effect" occurs where a negative first perception is generalized to other aspects of the candidate. Again, without specific information regarding that aspect of the candidate. The horns effect has tripped-up many candidates that have great eligibility and suitability but didn't make a good first impression.

The problem with falling into like is that it is similar to any form of infatuation, it can evaporate with experience—which can lead to disappointment, or worse, bad delivery results. I suspect that we fell into like with Eric, the candidate for the IT company job discussed in the opening pages. Although several people interviewed the candidate, we did not have a coordinated approach to the interview. We all asked our own questions. The consensus was that he was a great guy; we liked him. Unfortunately, those feelings evaporated for the CEO once Eric started the job.

How can you avoid being overly influenced by likability? Don't just get an impression of whether you like the person; get a perspective on what it would be like to work with the person. You will only like to work with a person if you both like him and like how he performs the job. Make the distinction between forming a personal judgment of likability and interviewing the person for the job. How? Ask better questions!

Research has shown that you are less likely to be overly influenced by likability if you take a structured approach to the interview that focuses on job requirements. This will help you avoid the too casual interview that is filled with the kind of banter that can heighten likability but does not give a perspective on what it would be like to work with the person day to day. Put your first impressions to the test during the interview. As you do, you may find that the halo or the horns disappear. Here are some strategies on how to take a structured approach to interviewing.

A job interview rarely lasts longer than an hour; the impact of the interview can last for years. Because interviews require an investment of both time and cost, you certainly want to get a good return on your investment by getting a meaningful assessment. Here are five tips that will help you structure your interview successfully and ask good questions.

Five Tips for Successful Interviews

Tip 1: Know What You're Looking For

The first step in creating a structure for an interview is to know where you want to go with the interview. Working the People Equation before you interview will help you take that important first step.

By developing the numerator to the People Equation, you will be clear about both the nonnegotiable activities you want performed and the outcomes you are looking for; in short, what you need. Your expectations of people and peoples' expectation of themselves are important factors in how well people perform their work. If you are clear regarding your needs and expectations, you can then structure the interview to assess whether you think a candidate will live up to your expectations.

By developing the suitability component in the denominator of the People Equation, you will know the traits and qualities that you are looking for—you will know your secret sauce. If you are clear about the traits you seek, you can structure the interview to determine whether the person gives strong evidence of those traits.

Tip 2: Ask Better Questions

Two types of questions increase the dependability of an interview: situational questions and behavioral questions that focus on job performance. Situational questions ask candidates how they would handle particular job-related situations. Behavioral questions ask candidates to describe a situation they encountered in their past and how they handled it. Situational interviews are based on the assumption that intentions predict behavior. Behavioral interviews are based on the assumption that past behavior is the best predictor of future behavior: that we are likely to repeat past behavior. Although there are strong advocates for both formats, several studies show that there is a negligible difference between the successes of the two approaches. I actually like to use both situational and behavior-based questions in an interview.

Before you interview, develop situational and/or behavior-based questions that relate to what you are looking for.

• Again, situational interview questions ask a candidate to describe what he would do in a hypothetical situation. For example, when interviewing someone for a sales position you might ask, "Imagine you are on a sales call and someone objects because the price is too high. How would you handle that situation?" Or, if you were interviewing someone for a project management position, you might ask, "Imagine you were in a situation where your team was under a lot of time pressure to complete a project you are managing. How would you handle the situation?"

• Behavior-based interview questions ask a candidate what she did in a specific situation. For the sales position you might ask, "Think of a situation you encountered where a prospective customer objected because the price was too high. Describe the situation and how you overcame the objection." Or, for the project management position, you might ask, "Think of a situation where your team was under a lot of time pressure to complete a project you were managing. Tell me about the situation, your actions and the results you achieved."

You can also combine the approaches when you are framing your questions. For instance, your first question might be, "How would you handle a tough sale?" You can then drill down following this hypothetical question by asking questions about past behavior. For instance, "Can you give me some examples of how you handled tough sales in the past?"

You may get greater insight into a candidate by asking for an instance of past success or failure that is not job specific. An example of this type of introspective behavioral question is: "Tell me about a time in your life that you did something that gave you a sense of accomplishment or pride and that is not related to work." As you listen to the answer, you can assess whether the qualities that made the candidate successful in that situation would also contribute to success in your job.

Abbe O'Rourke is a strong proponent of not limiting your questions to the job. She has, over the years, built several high-performance teams for companies in the information technology sector. She says, "Introspective questions that are not job specific can be very powerful. When a person talks about something they are proud of, or something they love, that is not job related the answer is normally full of detail and honesty." Abbe shares the following experience as an example of the impact of this type of introspective question.

Abbe needed a logistics lead for an IT server deployment team she was managing. The successful candidate had to be able to stand firm with engineers to get scheduling done and have enough situational awareness to get concurrence across multiple IT teams that had some difficult personalities. Abbe's first questions for one candidate, Anna, were behavioral questions that were related to the job. Abbe felt that there was something more that she was not getting. So she asked Anna to share an accomplishment that was not related to work; maybe a hobby. That question turned an inconclusive interview into a positive hiring decision. Here's what happened.

Anna responded that she was an avid horseback rider and recounted that her greatest achievement was acquiring and training a horse with a very strong personality. The horse was considered so unruly and un-trainable that he was about to be sold at auction to be processed for meat. Anna not only bought, tamed and trained the horse, she ultimately won Reserve Grand Champion in the state competition. Being an accomplished horsewoman herself, Abbe realized that it took athletic skill, horsemanship and a great deal of political savvy to bring a horse with a prior bad reputation into the winner's circle. Abbe knew that the qualities and communication skills required to accomplish this goal would help Anna relate successfully with the strong engineers and difficult personalities she would deal with in the job. That proved to be the case. Anna was a great hire. Because of Anna and other great hires, Abbe's team delivered millions of dollars of cost savings to the company. Abbe further says, "Introspective questions reveal how the candidate thinks, teams (or not), solves problems, relates to management and authority, develops a process or overcomes challenges. I find that a single introspective question generally leads to natural follow-on questions that are relevant to the qualities that contribute to success in the job."

In the final analysis, you get better insight into a candidate if you ask better questions. You will get a better return on the time—and cost—you invest in an interview if you invest a little time before the interview to frame some good behavioral, situational and introspective questions. When you are asking introspective questions, remember to give the candidate some time; time to reflect and gather their thoughts before they answer. That's how you get to the detail and honesty Abbe O'Rourke gets from introspective questions.

Tip 3: Interview Your Top Performers

Once you have developed your questions, interview your top performers. You want to hire people who are like your top performers, so ask them to answer the questions. You will very likely find a great deal of similarity in the answers. Most importantly, you can benchmark a candidate's answers against the answers your high performers give.

I encourage you to develop rating scales based on how close a candidate's answer is to the answer given by your top performers. This brings a level of objectivity into the interview process. You're looking for consistency in ratings between the various people interviewing a candidate. If the ratings are not consistent then you need to explore why there is the variance. One reason you may find for a variance is that one or more of the interviewers did not know how to use the rating scale. Interviewers need to be trained on what represents a similar answer and how to score an answer.

Tip 4: Evaluate the Joy Factor

An additional line of questions is helpful in evaluating job suitability. The questions are based on the premise that we tend to do the things we like to do and avoid—as much as possible—the things we don't like to do. You can simply ask:

1. What was your favorite job?
2. What did you like about it?
3. What was your least favorite job?
4. What didn't you like about it?
5. Who was your favorite boss?
6. Why?
7. Who was your least favorite boss?
8. Why?

Then benchmark the answers against the job you are filling. Does your job look more like the person's favorite job or least favorite job? Does the person to whom he or she will report look more like the person's favorite boss or least favorite boss?

I find that people are very willing to tell me about what they didn't like in a job or about a boss who drove them nuts. If I was interviewing the character Vince Vaughn played in *The Break-up,* you might hear him say, "They made me wash dishes and actually expected me to like it. Can you believe that? It was miserable standing on my feet all day. And the boss, I don't even want to go there!" Sorry Vince, not a good fit for my job.

Asking behavioral questions can also help you gain some insight into the situational awareness dimension of suitability. One element of situational awareness is how you manage your relationships with others. To get some insight into that aspect of situational awareness, you can ask a candidate to describe his best working relationship and what made it work. You can also ask the candidate to describe a working relationship that was not good and why he thinks it didn't work.

Tip 5: Check the Halo

Although first impressions are fallible, they may be sound. A candidate's halo may still be intact at the end of the interview. A candidate's halo is still intact if the interview ends and you can say, "I liked her and I liked her response to the questions." First impression validated. The halo is tarnished if you say, "I liked her, but didn't like her response to the questions." That's the person who you like but with whom you would not like to work. The interview infatuation may soon fade.

One of the great benefits of a structured interview is that it can sometimes turn horns into halos. At the end of the interview you might find yourself saying, "At first I didn't like her, but I liked her answers to the questions." Negative first impressions are hard to overcome, but there can be big payoffs. The cofounders of Google offer a great story about the value of overcoming first impressions.

Google cofounders, Larry Page and Sergey Brin, became overnight billionaires when Google initially went public with an astounding opening stock price of $135 per share. An interesting part of their story is that each says he initially found the other to be obnoxious when they met at Stanford. Had they gone their separate ways based on first impressions it would have cost them about $6 billion.

There is wisdom in the old adage, "You can't judge a book by its cover." But we all do. Following the Five Tips for Successful Interviews will help you see what's inside the book—help you judge the applicant's suitability for the job along with his or her eligibility. It may be just as great or bad as you initially expected. But you might be surprised. The book you didn't think you would like at first may turn out to be a pretty good read.

People Equation Quotient:
High Performance Potential

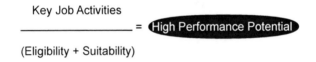

Key Job Activities
————————————— = High Performance Potential
(Eligibility + Suitability)

JUST AS A MATHEMATICAL EQUATION is designed to help you solve a math problem, the People Equation is designed to help you solve the problem of identifying high performance potential so you can avoid the consequences of a bad hire or promotion. "High performance potential" is the quotient of the People Equation. So let's apply the People Equation to a problem. This will show how evaluating eligibility and suitability in the context of key job activities can give insight into the kind of high performance potential that will translate into job success.

The construction services company discussed earlier was faced with the problem of replacing a production manager for one of the company's most profitable offices. The production manager position is clearly an "A" position for the company: a production manager has major direct impact on customer satisfaction, efficiency and company profitability.

So how do we apply the People Equation to this mission-critical talent decision? Following the next six steps will help you get the People Equation right. You will see that filling the job for the production manager turned out to be somewhat of a Cinderella story.

Step 1: Identify Nonnegotiable Activities

The company identified the following activities as nonnegotiable activities for a production manager:

1. Manage superintendents.
2. Maintain consistent field interaction with the builder community and interface with builders directly when necessary to resolve construction problems.
3. Manage warehouse personnel.
4. Make adjustments in inventory to reflect demand.

Step 2: Define Measurements for Nonnegotiable Activities

Management-related activities are the majority of the activities involved in the production manager job—and most management jobs for that matter. One measurement of success for a production manager is the success of the people he manages. Are the superintendents he manages meeting the performance standards set out in their job description? By way of example, let's revisit Ben's NASCAR race contest to measure results.

By entering the superintendents in a NASCAR race to track their punch list performance against the standard, Ben found a fun way to measure a nonnegotiable activity. The results of the race each week show that the superintendents he manages are meeting performance standards for the punch list activity. If you measure Ben's performance as a manager by the performance of his team, Ben measures up. He manages a winning team that meets the company objectives through his leadership. We certainly want the new project manager to manage as well as Ben.

The production manager job also includes both interaction with the builder community and resolving construction problems. How can you measure this kind of customer service activity? Surveying the customer—in this instance builders—is one way to evaluate if a production manager is measuring up to expectations. You can also put measurements in place to track whether construction problems are both resolved and resolved in a timely manner.

By defining the job we know what activities are required; by putting measurements in place we know what success in the job looks like. A production manager must have the eligibility and suitability to perform the nonnegotiable activities to a measured standard of performance.

Step 3: Establish Eligibility Requirements

What kind of education, training, skill and experience are required to perform the nonnegotiable activities well? Because the production management job is a technical job, specific training and trade certifications are required. The company is also looking for someone with a minimum of four years in direct supervision, but would prefer five or more years of experience. Remember to think about both minimum requirements and optimum, or preferred, requirements when establishing eligibility requirements. Optimally, the company would like the production manager to have been a superintendent with the company for a couple of years. Satisfying this last eligibility requirement would mean that the company would need to promote from within.

There are also the "preferred but not required" aspects of eligibility. The company would, for instance, prefer some experience with inventory but that experience is not required. Why? Because the company has successfully trained production managers to perform the inventory-related activities of the job.

Step 4: Define and Assess for Suitability

The person who is suitable for the production manager job is a person who enjoys the activities involved in the job—has the joy factor—and also has the situational awareness needed to be successful in the job. The company, for instance, is looking for a person who enjoys and has the traits that support problem-solving. Traits like being naturally analytical and having an inherent tendency to scrutinize the potential difficulties in a plan of action. The company is looking for a person with initiative and who will persist in the face of obstacles. The company is looking for a person who both wants to lead and has the personal traits that support good leadership and customer interaction. Interpersonal traits like good communication, natural helpfulness and desire to enlist cooperation. Advances in assessment technology provide an effective way to evaluate these hard-to-gauge types of traits and inclinations. The construction services company relies on an assessment to collect the data it needs to assess the traits and natural inclinations that dictate job suitability.

Again, one of the advantages of assessment data is that it can tell you what's in the secret sauce—the traits that are shared by high performers in a particular job in your company. We determined that one of the ingredients in the secret sauce for the production manager job is a very strong tendency to place and maintain order. All of the top performing production managers for the company are very highly organized. They love organizing. The tendency to be organized is a suitability trait. Certainly, organizing skills can be taught. You can teach someone to do an activity; it's hard to teach someone to love an activity. A person with a natural desire to organize and be organized—a person who loves organizing—has the highest performance potential. Skills help you perform an activity; natural desire motivates you to excel in the activity. There is value in capitalizing on a person's natural traits and talents.

The company first looked in its most tenured ranks to find a superintendent with the traits in the secret sauce. The goal was to hire from within. Several eligible candidates were identified. Unfortunately, they did not prove to be suitable. They were lacking in some of the interpersonal traits that were shared by top performers. Assessment data showed that they lacked the needed situational awareness. So the company cast the net further. That's where this becomes a bit of a Cinderella story.

There was a superintendent, Allan, who had only been with the company 18 months, although he had 3 years of prior experience as a superintendent. The CEO said, "Allan had not been with the company long enough to be on my radar screen." Just like Cinderella, Allan came out of relative obscurity because assessment data identified him as having the secret sauce. Allan's production manager confirmed that he was doing a very good job. The CEO interviewed Allan and was very impressed. Although Allan did not satisfy all of the optimum eligibility requirements, the company determined that he had enough eligibility. That combined with outstanding suitability resulted in an offer.

How is Allan doing? Does he have the performance potential we thought he had? Yes. He has had some challenges that reflected his level of experience. But senior management is very pleased with his performance, which continues to improve as he matures in the position. The builders like him and his superintendents are performing to standards. More experience would have been a plus, but Allan's strong suitability traits have supported success.

Step 5: Strike the Right Balance Between Eligibility and Suitability

The production manager job is technical. It requires a good deal of subject matter expertise to effectively manage superintendents and resolve construction problems. It also requires good organizing and interpersonal traits. It's one of the jobs that require a relatively equal balance of eligibility and suitability to be successful.

Step 6: Conduct a Structured Interview

The CEO was impressed with Allan during the interview. Not only did Allan have great suitability and solid, if not optimum, eligibility, he also passed the likability test. He had earned a halo after a structured interview. The interview confirmed that there was a good fit with the job and a good fit with the company. Remember the five tips we discussed for conducting a structured interview:

1. Know what you are looking for.
2. Ask better questions (ask behavioral, situational and introspective questions).
3. Interview your top performers.
4. Evaluate the joy factor.
5. Finally, check the halo.

The six steps the company went through in applying the People Equation provide the path to discover high performance potential. You can think of them as the six steps for getting the right person in the right job.

---------------------------CR·RD---------------------------

**Six Steps for Getting the Right Person
in the Right Job**
Step 1: Identify nonnegotiable job activities.
Step 2: Define measurements for the activities.
Step 3: Establish eligibility requirements.
Step 4: Define and assess for suitability.
Step 5: Strike the right balance between
eligibility and suitability.
Step 6: Conduct a structured interview.

Following these six steps leads to the understanding of the activities and requirements of the job as well as the personal qualities you need to consider in order to select your next top performer. Following the analytical framework the People Equation articulates has helped me and my clients diminish the impact of personal bias and make better talent decisions.

As we close Part 1 of the book, I would like to make some observations about biases. We all bring personal biases to a talent decision. By acknowledging your biases, they won't trip you up in the hiring process. For instance, I have a bias in regard to sales that, unmanaged, could trip me up.

I like relationship selling. I even provide training on how to build a great relationship and great return at same time.

I have a bias in favor of the personal traits that engender long-term relationships. But long-term relationships are not the desired outcomes of many sales jobs. Many sales jobs presume that the customer will buy only once. I personally like complex sales. But a quick close is important to success in many sales positions. As noted earlier, many sales jobs require little or no technical background, while others require the salesperson to be a technical expert. Granted, the ability to persuade is a personal quality that is needed in order to be suitable for any sales job. But beyond that, it is a function of the specific sales job.

The key is not to look at a job through your personal biases; rather, approach the job analytically using the steps in the People Equation. That way you will identify the people who have the personal qualities that promote success *in the specific job* you want them to do.

I help a client select salespeople for a sales job that requires limited technical background and a quick close. The secret sauce for that position contains personal qualities that are very different from those for which I have a bias. Fortunately my bias is irrelevant because we make the decision based on the analytical framework of the People Equation: we follow the six steps. A shared analytical framework together with reliable, job-specific assessment data, elevates the decision-making process for selecting salespeople to the same level of objectivity as would be expected in other critical business decisions regarding, for example, capital or operational efficiency.

We often hear that people are a company's greatest asset. In fact, the **right people** in the **right jobs** are a company's greatest asset. I trust that the People Equation will help you get the right people in the right jobs because it shows you the steps to take to identify high performance potential.

Once you get the right people in the right jobs, you have to keep them. That's the rest of the story and the purpose of Part 2 of this book.

PART 2

The Rest of the Story:
Motivation and Job Success

High Performance Potential

Job Success

"TAKE THIS JOB and shove it / I ain't working here no more." Those lyrics from a David Allan Coe song sum up how a lot of people feel about their jobs. White collar. Blue collar. It doesn't make any difference. In many cases, it isn't about the job itself. Research suggests that a majority of people actually like the kind of work they do. It's the people they work for or the culture of the company that is often the problem.

One way to think about People Equation is that getting the People Equation right is a starting point. Once you get the right people in the right jobs, you have to keep them. There are management practices that motivate employees to say, "I want to work here." Or, "I want to work for you." I have found that the following five management practices result in employee satisfaction, create a good working environment and build a strong culture:

1. Compensation

2. Appreciation

3. Communication

4. Opportunity to Stretch and Grow

5. Fun

Managers who follow these practices are able to tap into the natural motivation of high potential employees. They are managers who have *motivational competency*. Managers with motivational competency act in ways that directly and positively impact the success of employees and organizations. In this part of the book, we will explore how to implement these five management practices in ways that will help you develop your motivational competency.

David Ogilvy was a master of motivational competency. Take another look at the introduction to his recruiting brochure:

"If you join Ogilvy & Mather, we shall teach you
everything we know about advertising. We shall
pay you well, and do our damnedest to make
you succeed. If you show promise, we shall load
responsibility on you—fast. Life in our agency
can be very exciting. You will never be bored. It's
tough, but it's fun."[29]

David Ogilvy's leadership is not remembered because of
what he wrote, but because of what he did. He is remembered as a man of action and not mere words. He didn't just
make Ogilvy & Mather sound like a great place to work;
he did what it took to make it a great place to work. In his
article, "The House that Ogilvy Built," Kenneth Roman describes Ogilvy as a leader who set an excellent example, who
treated people well, helped them succeed and used training
to help his employees learn how to treat people well. Ogilvy
saw culture as a competitive differentiator. After reading a
book on culture in 1985, Ogilvy talked about culture in an
address to the Agency's board of directors:

"'Apparently we have a very strong culture. *Indeed, it may be this, more than anything else that
differentiates us from our competitors.*' It starts
with the working atmosphere, he said: 'Some of

our people spend their entire working lives in our company. We do our damnedest to make it a *happy* experience for them."[30]

He clearly understood the ramifications of the kind of working atmosphere your daily actions and management practices create.

If Roman is typical of an Ogilvy hire, Ogilvy succeeded in making work a good experience. Roman started working for David Ogilvy in 1963, eventually leading the firm as Chairman and CEO before going on to consult, serve on other boards and pen several books. Years later, Roman still writes about Ogilvy with warmth and admiration. He observes that David Ogilvy left a remarkable legacy in advertising, but that his most enduring legacy is as an "institution builder."[31]

To get the People Equation right, you have to master the managerial competencies that create a good working environment. David Ogilvy used his motivational competency to do just that. You can too. You will develop your motivational competency as you master the five management practices we will explore in this part of the book.

Not only will developing your motivational competency help you create a good work environment and retain top talent, it's good for the bottom line. Since 1998

Fortune magazine and the Great Place to Work Institute have conducted annual surveys of publicly traded companies to find the 100 best places to work in corporate America. What is interesting is that the 100 Best Companies have delivered long-term financial performance that is notably superior to that of comparable companies. Alex Edmans, Assistant Professor of Finance at Wharton, researched the financial performance of the *Fortune* best places to work. Edmans concludes that companies with a high level of employee satisfaction produce superior long-term returns.[32]

I encourage you to think about employee satisfaction broadly. The practical definition of an "employee" is changing today as more companies hire contract and part time workers. Today, many employees and contract workers work remotely. A high level of motivational competency is required to tap into the full performance potential of these workers by creating an inclusive working environment. As we now explore each of the five management practices in detail, think about how these management practices can also apply to contract and part-time workers as well as employees working remotely.

Let's take a look at each of the five management practices that create a high level of employee satisfaction.

Five Key Management Practices that Create Motivational Competency

Practice 1: Compensation

Let's take a look at compensation. Are you, for the most part, doing the work you do because of what it pays? Second question: Are the people you work with—or who work for you—working mostly because of what the job pays?

Let's see how your answers compare to research. Would you be surprised to find that in an experiment conducted by Chip Heath that participants ranked motivators like pay as their own top incentive only 22 percent of the time? By contrast, they thought others would rank it much higher; in some instances they thought 85 percent would give it the top slot.[33] That experiment suggests that we tend to greatly overestimate how much other people are motivated by pay. In order to master the motivational competency regarding compensation, you first have to have a realistic view of compensation as a motivator.

Frankly, money is generally way up there on the list of motivators; even if it is not necessarily the dominant motivator. In Heath's experiment, money was the dominate factor for only 22 percent of the participants. That doesn't mean that it was not very important for the remaining 78 percent. A good litmus test is: are employees "satisfied" with their pay?

To exercise good managerial competency, you need to be able to determine what creates pay satisfaction. Some of the things that researchers have identified as playing a part in satisfaction—or dissatisfaction—with pay include:

- Is my pay on par with what other companies pay for similar work?

- Does my pay increase year-over-year? (It is important to employees that their standard of living does not go down. People tend to get disappointed if a pay increase is less than an increase they previously received; they can get upset if pay does not increase to keep pace with increases in cost of living.)

- Is my pay consistent with contribution?

- Is my pay on par with other employees in the company?

- Is my pay fair relative to the overall profitability of the company?

These are the kinds of things you need to think about if you are going to tap into what people really think about pay. They are some of the determinants of pay satisfaction identified by David Sirota, Louis Mischkind and Michael

Meltzer in their extensive research on employee compensation. Their research is discussed at length in their book *The Enthusiastic Employee, How Companies Profit by Giving Workers What They Want.*[34] What stands out is the strong connection between pay and fairness. Am I being paid fairly in comparison to others in my field and within the company? Is there an equitable distribution of the profits of the company? It is basically a matter of trust and fairness. Being able to trust a company to treat you fairly in regard to pay promotes job satisfaction. The authors of *The Enthusiastic Employee* found that whether employees accept pay cuts as legitimate depends on whether employees trust management. They note, "When trust is present, the kind of support an organization can receive from its workers is absolutely amazing."[35]

In my experience, most companies lay a good foundation for fair pay because they understand the importance that compensation plays in getting and keeping high performers. But pay alone is generally not enough to keep employees fully engaged. To develop real motivational competency, you also have to understand that appreciation, communication and the opportunity to stretch, grow and have fun also have a significant impact on job satisfaction.

Practice 2: Appreciation

Appreciation in business is one of the most powerful ways to motivate employees to give you their best. Appreciation is high impact, low cost and, regrettably, more the exception than the rule. Importantly, appreciation is an expression of a value mindset. Let me explain.

There is a natural tendency in business to focus on problems: what's going wrong and what people are doing wrong. And we should. We need to both identify problems and be good at solving problems. We need a problem mindset. But an exclusive focus on what people are doing wrong or not doing is myopic. To be most effective we also need to focus on what is going right. It's like the paradoxes we discussed regarding developing good situational awareness: you need to strike a good balance between a problem mindset and a value mindset. I view appreciation as the expression of a value mindset because it is the way we acknowledge that someone is adding value by doing something right—the same way we express appreciation to our customers for the value they bring to our business. To express appreciation we first have to be looking for what is going right.

Let's take a look at why developing a value mindset—looking for what is going right—and expressing appreciation is high impact, low cost and, regrettably, usually the exception rather than the rule.

Appreciation Has High Impact

Bottom line: we all like appreciation. To receive "sincere" recognition for an accomplishment is among the most fundamental of human needs. When you were a child didn't you want your parents' praise when you did something good at school? Has it really changed now that you are an adult? Don't you still want recognition when you do something good at work? Statistics suggest that most of us still do. Several sources of data show that a lack of appreciation or recognition is the number one reason people quit their jobs!

"Simply put, when employees know that their strengths and potential will be praised and recognized, they are significantly more likely to produce value,"[36] report Adrian Gostick and Chester Elton in their book *The Carrot Principle*. They back it up with comprehensive data linking appreciation and recognition to improved return on equity, improved return on assets and improved operating margins.

The authors of *The Carrot Principle* collaborated with The Jackson Organization in a study of 26,000 employees at all levels in 31 organizations. They found that companies that ""recognized excellence" had both a return on equity and return on assets that were more than three times higher than companies that did not recognize excellence. Operating margins were also significantly higher.[37] Karen Endresen, Ph.D., of The Jackson Organization, made the following comment regarding the research: "Up until this study, the link between recognition and financial performance was largely anecdotal. Recognition was considered by some to be an emotional afterthought, while those who believed that effective recognition would drive results had no hard data to prove it. This study took recognition results from myth to reality—from the soft side of business to a proven business essential."[38]

The distinction Dr. Endresen makes between considering recognition as an "emotional afterthought" versus a "proven business essential" is a key point. Considering the impact that a lack of recognition can have on both retention and profitability, it is important to ask yourself: "How effective am I at giving sincere recognition?" Is expressing appreciation an emotional afterthought for you or a consistent day-to-day practice? It is a consistent day-to-day practice for those who have developed strong motivational competency.

Low Cost

The great thing about appreciation is that it doesn't cost you anything and you can start immediately. What I'm talking about here is informal appreciation or recognition; the day-to-day appreciation that a manager can give when she sees something good going on. It motivates an employee when he hears personally from his manager that his performance is appreciated.

Generic appreciation, while it is certainly nice, is not the same as individual appreciation. A conversation I recently had with Lance, the CEO of a mid-market services company, illustrates the point. One of his managers and the manager's team had done a very good job. The manager had put forward above-and-beyond effort to achieve a very big win. As we talked about the win, I wondered if an expression of appreciation might be a great idea. Lance said, "Absolutely. I just did that. I sent the team an e-mail thanking them and congratulating them on a great win." In addition, I encouraged him to offer specific appreciation to his manager. He got the point and did it. Two interesting things followed.

Although Lance had gotten "thanks" e-mails in response to the first e-mail, he got a very grateful and lengthy response to the second e-mail. In her lengthy response, the manager said that the team could not have achieved the win without Debra, a key member of his team. The manager had expressed her personal appreciation to Debra, but said that she was sure Debra would value an acknowledgment from Lance. Off went another e-mail of appreciation. Lance called me to share that he had received a very heartwarming e-mail response from Debra. He said, "This feels really good. There's something to this personal appreciation thing." Lance is a successful leader. One reason he's successful is that he is always looking for ways to be a better leader. This series of e-mails took his managerial competency up a notch. The point is that appreciation needs to be given for both group and individual performance. As the old adage goes, "Praise often, praise specifically."

Exception Rather Than the Rule

How often have you received appreciation for what you achieve at work? How often do you express personal appreciation to the people who work for you? You are having a typical work experience if receiving and expressing appreciation are more the exception than the rule for you. Why don't we see more appreciation in companies if appreciation has high impact and doesn't cost anything? One reason is that very few managers are consciously looking at what's going right day in and day out. They have developed the necessary problem mindset but have not developed the ability to strike a good balance between looking at problems and looking at what's going right. Why is that?

I have concluded that a possible root cause is that many, maybe most, leaders and managers are very hard on themselves. Because we tend to relate to others the way we relate to ourselves, it stands to reason that if you think critically of yourself you will tend to think critically of others. My conclusion is based on Harrison Assessment data I have reviewed over the last eight years. A majority of the senior executives, managers and executive/managerial candidates I have reviewed tend to be very hard on themselves; in many cases hyper-critical. Although it is anecdotal information, rather than a formal research study by Dr. Harrison, it still gives insight into why giving appreciation is more the exception than the rule. Appreciation would tend to be an emotional afterthought if your primary thoughts are on what needs to improve in yourself and in others.

As I'm writing this, I just got off the phone with the District Sales Manager for a client. He is highly self-critical and was particularly hard on himself during the conversation. To try to shift his focus to a more balanced perspective, I asked him two questions. I first asked him, "What are a few things you would like to improve about yourself?" He started rattling things off. This kind of rapid machine gun response is typically what I hear when I ask that question. I then asked him, "What are a few things that you're doing really well?" Long pause. Again, very typical of what I experience when I ask that question. We finally did get a few pluses on the table, but it was unnatural for him. Again, it stands to reason that if he finds self-appreciation hard, it will be harder for him to naturally appreciate others. Because he wants to experience the high-impact, low-cost benefits of appreciation, he has made a conscious decision to look for and recognize good things that his people are doing. He has really made a conscious decision to treat others better than he currently treats himself. He has made the decision to develop a new habit of appreciation because he personally believes that the benefit to his long-term success outweighs the discomfort that often goes along with developing a new habit.

We've all experienced emotional resistance when we think about developing a new habit. Does this phrase sound familiar? "I know I should do it, *but* . . ." I hear a variety of "yea, buts" when I introduce the value of appreciation. As my colleague and friend, Nance Guilmartin, says in her book *The Power of Pause*, "After years of advising and teaching professionals, I've come to value those inevitable moments in the process of introducing new ideas when participants say, 'Yeah, but . . .'"[39] Let's consider a few of the common "yeah buts" I hear as reasons not to develop the habit of expressing sincere appreciation.

"Yeah, but if the people I hire need me to appreciate them to get them motivated, I've hired the wrong people." Of course you want to hire people that are naturally motivated to get the job done; that's what the People Equation is all about. High performers do tend to be highly self-motivated. We are not talking about motivating people to do a job; we are talking about motivating top performers to stay with you. Retention! Appreciating what your employees are doing well is simply part of a good retention strategy. Success looks like getting the right people, with the right skills in the right job *and keeping them.* Offering frequent appreciation helps you keep your top performers.

"Yeah, but I don't want to appreciate someone that is generally doing well but not living up to all of my expectations." This concern again misses the point of giving appreciation. Appreciation reinforces behaviors that you want to see repeated. It is a form of positive reinforcement. If there is an area where you are not satisfied with a person's performance, for instance, appreciating that person's efforts to improve will tend to positively motivate that person to continue to improve.

When discussing this with a manufacturing exec, he said: "I get it. It's the same thing I'm doing to teach my three-year-old son to get dressed by himself. If at first he can only do his socks, I give him praise for that. I hope it will eventually lead to him getting dressed by himself." I'm certainly not suggesting that we treat the people who work for us like they are three years old. I am suggesting that, like this exec, we can all find some personal experience where we have used appreciation to motivate someone to continue to improve; we've praised the good accomplished and encouraged someone to achieve more. That personal experience can provide a great point of reference. It can help you see how to also use appreciation as a motivator in your work life.

One of my favorite "yeah buts" is: "but they will come to expect it." That's exactly what you want. You want people to come to work expecting that their efforts will be valued and appreciated.

Feeling uncomfortable expressing praise may be at the root of your personal "yeah buts." If so, ask yourself: What kind of appreciation am I comfortable giving? Although expressing appreciation or recognition face to face or in a telephone call is the most effective approach, you just may not be comfortable expressing appreciation in person. If you can't get comfortable, find an alternative way to express appreciation. An e-mail or note for instance. The key is to start noticing what is going right and find a way that you are comfortable sincerely acknowledging it.

There are a couple of additional tips that will help you get the most impact from giving appreciation: be sincere and be timely—do it on the spot if you can. As Ken

Blanchard says regarding people who work for you, "Catch them doing things right."[40]

In Louisiana we have a concept called "lagniappe." "Lagniappe" means an unexpected bonus; a little something extra. If you are highly critical of yourself, there is lagniappe in adopting a habit of appreciating others. As you consistently recognize what others are doing right, you may find that you actually begin to recognize more of what you are doing right. I often see self-appreciation grow as an unexpected consequence of developing the value mindset it takes to catch others doing something right.

Practice 3: Communication

"Most managers know from experience that employees get more pumped when they understand where the company is going, why, and what role they play in getting there." This is a comment Jack Welch made in a *Business Week* column in which he advocates the need for transparency when communicating change.[41] Everyone knows communication is essential. Are you communicating in a way that gets people engaged—"more pumped up" as Welch says—or are you are creating "ouch points"?

The concept of an "ouch point" is not original to me, but I think it is a great concept. Actually, the Opinion

Research Corporation publishes an *Ouch Point Series* that addresses frustrations Americans face in a variety of scenarios in their personal and work lives. One "ouch point" that topped the list of a recent *Ouch Point Survey* is poor communication from management.[42] That survey also indicates that employees are twice as likely to "go the extra mile" for a company if they are satisfied with the ways in which the company communicates difficult decisions. Similarly, AUMPartners' research on the impact of the 2008–2009 financial crisis on investment firms reveals that "candor has become the largest gap in terms of what investment professionals want and what they believe they currently have in their organizations."[43] AUMPartners provides research and consulting to investment firms. They found that there was a significant decline in open and candid communication in investment firms during the crisis period and that the lack of open and candid communication became the single greatest unmet need of employees in that sector. Ouch. Masters of motivational competency know that candid communication is important all the time and essential during a crisis. Transparency in communication is about keeping people in the loop. Keeping employees in the loop can avoid an "ouch point" that can make employees disengage.

There are three additional communication ouch points that create disengagement:

1. Failure to clearly communicate performance expectations.

2. Failure to communicate about performance on a regular basis.

3. Failure to listen.

Let's take a look at how to avoid an "ouch" regarding each of these points.

Clearly Communicate Performance Expectations

If you have defined the numerator in the People Equation, you have successfully positioned yourself to clearly communicate performance expectations. You have defined the outcomes you are looking for, the nonnegotiable activities the employee is expected to undertake and how you will measure and validate performance. It is important to remember to communicate that to the employee.

Alex is a case in point. Alex had been hired as an operations manager and was under-performing as he approached 90 days into the job. The COO of the company was surprised because they had applied the People Equation and Alex appeared to be both highly suited and eligible for the job. As the COO began to try to figure out why Alex was not living up to expectations he discovered an onboarding problem. The Director of Operations, Alex's boss, was very busy solving a customer problem when Alex started. He had only generally communicated the outcomes, activities and measures. Ouch. In his first 90 days Alex had not had much access to the Director of Operations because the Director found it necessary to spend a lot of time on the customer site in another city. Alex had been figuring it out for himself based on his prior experience and asking questions of his coworkers and team. There was one metric on which he was expected to focus that he had not discovered. That metric was determined to be the root of the performance issue. Once he understood what was expected, he immediately began to deliver. It wasn't really a problem with Alex; it was a problem with onboarding.

"Onboarding" is a term for orientation practices: taking defined steps to assimilate new employees to help them deliver results faster. There are a lot of practices that help orient an employee and accelerate the ability of an employee to hit the deck running. Clearly communicating expectations is a fundamental onboarding practice. Every job has expected activities and outcomes, and every company has its own set of procedures, practices and traditions. Don't make new employees learn these things the hard way like Alex. It's potentially highly de-motivating for the employee and impacts performance. Clearly communicating expectations will reduce your own and the employee's frustration level and may even save you money.

Let's quantify the financial impact of the "ouch." There is an interesting research study done by IDC, a global provider of market intelligence. In their study of 400 US and UK corporations, IDC found that employee misunderstanding costs these corporations an estimated $37 billion from their EBITDA (earnings before interest, depreciation and taxes). "Employee misunderstanding" is defined as "actions or errors of omission by employees who have misunderstood or misinterpreted (or were misinformed about) company policies, business processes, job function or a combination of the three."[44] By reducing misunderstanding (communicating clearly), you can potentially reduce costs as well as reduce frustration—yours and your employee's—and ramp up performance quicker.

Communicate About Performance on a Regular Basis

How am I doing? That's a question we all have. Feedback is essential to all of us as we endeavor to grow and perform well. It's how we determine if we are on track and doing well—or not. One kind of feedback is expressing appreciation for what someone is doing right—for a job well done. Although, as human beings, we tend to prefer praise to criticism, that does not mean we don't want constructive feedback on where we need to improve.

Another word for giving feedback about where I need to improve is "guidance." I like the term "guidance" because it implies more than just providing performance information. It implies giving me direction on the steps I can take to improve. It's about helping me succeed. As David Ogilvy wrote in his recruiting brochure, "[We will] do our damnedest to make you succeed."

The goal of feedback—appreciation for what I'm doing right and guidance about where I need to improve—is to enhance performance. In order to enhance performance the feedback has to be regular. In the day-to-day press of business, too many managers lose sight of how important it is to give ongoing feedback. They wait until a serious problem develops before stepping in to provide guidance. Ouch. By providing regular feedback you can prevent problems from becoming serious by catching them before they escalate.

Some managers also operate under the illusion that top performers don't need guidance because they are top performers; top performers know how to take care of themselves. They probably do, but we all benefit from guidance. There is a tendency to spend time with lower performing employees rather than with top performers. You may get a better return on your time investment by spending more time giving guidance to your "A" players.

Guidance not only needs to be regular, it also needs to be constructive. To make sure it is constructive, it should be based on facts and behavior and also involve two-way communication. One of the tests of a good working relationship is the ability to discuss performance issues constructively. Managers with a high level of motivational competency use opportunities to give guidance as a means to build a stronger relationship with an employee. They realize that providing guidance and listening to their employee are really valuable ways of paying attention to an employee; and in the final analysis, paying attention is highly motivating.

Listen

Experience has taught me that one of the most powerful practices in business—and life—is the practice of listening in a way that results in understanding. Our need to be understood is one of our most basic needs. It is at the root of an interesting communication paradox: you can actually motivate more successfully by listening than you can by speaking. In 1990 I got clear feedback that I was not a master of this paradox.

In 1990 I was the CEO of a natural gas marketing and trading company. That year I took part in a week-long executive leadership development program. In advance of the program, all of my direct reports were asked to fill out a questionnaire on my leadership qualities, and I filled out the same questionnaire. There were several questions on how effectively I listened to them. When I filled out the questionnaire, I gave myself a reasonably high score because I thought I listened fairly well. My peoples' answers were provided to me anonymously during the program. They did not agree with my assessment of my listening skills. Nobody gave me a particularly high score. Ouch. Once I picked my ego up off the floor, I realized I was receiving important feedback. What was interesting—but, nonetheless a sad commentary—was that *none* of the executives participating in the program had received high scores. And there were some fairly high profile leaders in the program.

It was clear that I needed to develop better listening skills. So I began to learn and practice reflective listening. I found the effect to be, well, remarkable. I discovered that when I listened to someone to a point of understanding, that person typically tended to want to listen to me. Listening reflectively improved my impact as a leader. It also helped me get better results when negotiating and selling. It's actually a fairly simple process.

To listen reflectively, simply pause and rephrase what you heard—put it in your own words. Yes, it's that simple. Even though it's simple, it may feel awkward at first. Just like any new skill, it takes some practice. It's like driving a car with a standard transmission.

If you have had the experience of driving a standard, it probably felt very awkward at first when you had to pause, take your foot off the gas and then press the clutch in to shift gears. But after a while you got into the rhythm and you did it without even thinking about it. Practicing the discipline to pause and check in to make sure you understand is no different. You will eventually get into a natural listening sequence that includes listen, pause, confirm your understanding and then respond. It is far more impactful than the usual listening pattern of listen and immediately respond.

You may find a lead-in helpful as you start to confirm your understanding. For instance, you might say, "If I understand you, _____." Fill in the blank by rephrasing or summarizing what you understood in your own words. Again, here is the sequence:

1. Listen

2. Pause

3. Confirm your understanding. Rephrase:
   "If I understand you, _____."

4. Respond

When you pause and rephrase what you heard, you will likely discover that you didn't quite understand. That's alright. It's reality! The interesting thing is that if you are sincerely trying to understand someone, that person will help you.

Telephone numbers, for instance, are an area where many people commonly practice reflective listening. I give you my telephone number. You pause to repeat it. Oops. You got it wrong. I quickly correct you by giving you the right number. Regardless of what you are talking about, the person you are speaking with will likely clarify your understanding if you didn't fully understand them—just like when you get a telephone number wrong. Remember, the person to whom you are listening has a strong need to be understood.

Another interesting thing about reflective listening is that it cuts down on the internal conversations we tend to have when we appear to be listening. It is very common to be thinking about how we are going to respond—the next point we want to make—while we are listening. These internal conversations inhibit understanding. We are not fully listening to what is being said if we are having internal conversations. But what if there is a test of your understanding? If you are about to put your understanding to the test by rephrasing what you think I said, would you be more likely to focus on what I'm saying rather than on your next point? Most of us do pay closer attention when we practice reflective listening. As a result, the people to whom you are listening can usually feel that they have your full attention—because they do.

As I said, reflective listening has a big payoff. The benefits I have experienced as a result of practicing reflective listening over the years have made me passionate about sharing the process. Teaching reflective listening has been a core part of the negotiation, sales and leadership programs I have provided for 15 years. The participants in my programs over the years have not been any different than the participants in that leadership program in which I participated in 1990. Very few listen effectively. It appears that the ability to listen to the point of understanding seldom comes naturally to us. It certainly didn't for me. But I have seen over and over again that it becomes natural very quickly with some consistent practice. You will very likely discover that you enhance your ability to build both deep rapport and create trust as you learn to listen reflectively. In short, you will increase your motivational competency.

Practice 4: Opportunity to Stretch and Grow

We are all born with an intense desire to learn—to grow and develop. Everyone reading this book at some point defied gravity and learned to walk. Although the intensity to grow and develop diminishes for some as they mature, it remains in all of us to a lesser or greater degree. You will find that the desire to grow and develop remains intense for many of your top performers. Success for them involves challenging and stretching themselves—continually improving. If they have a very intense achievement mindset, they do not just seek challenge, they thrive on it. The bigger the challenge, the more they will stretch. Part of developing motivational competency is to recognize the need to grow and then providing opportunity for growth—opportunity to stretch and achieve in a work environment.

High-level jobs typically attract people with an intense desire to grow. That desire is not limited to high-level jobs. I learned that lesson in a humbling experience early in my career as a business consultant. It was a lesson taught by bellmen at a boutique hotel.

My colleague, Nance Guilmartin, and I had been hired to help a prominent boutique hotel achieve four-diamond status from three-diamond status. We developed a customer service training program to help the hotel achieve its goal. We began delivering the program at the top and then cascaded it down the various levels of the organization. As we got to the bellmen, we considered whether we should simplify the program. We decided not to. That proved to be a wise decision.

As we began the training we were introduced to a group of people who loved serving customers, understood their needs and had great ideas for improving service. The bellmen position in this hotel was an "A" position. The bellmen were the first people the guests encountered. They were full of great ideas on how to deliver four-diamond service. We discovered that management did not get a lot of their front-line feedback; it got blocked by their supervisors. Here's where my lesson in humility comes in: the bellmen were the most engaged and appreciative of all of the groups that went through the training. They were quick to both get it and apply it. They expressed their appreciation to management for investing in them. The owners and management of the hotel and I had misjudged the bellmen and the position; we learned a big lesson that improved our motivational competency—and the stature of the hotel.

When the secret guest came to review the hotel, the secret guest received four-diamond service and the hotel got its fourth diamond. That secret guest was no doubt greeted by a bellman with an intense desire to learn and a joy in service. It could have been Mario. Mario had a love of life; the kind of enthusiasm that is infectious. And he loved being a bellman at the hotel. We struck up a friendship and communicated for several years following our work with the hotel. I once asked him why he liked being a bellman. To my surprise, he said because it was challenging. "How so," I said. He then gave me a great lesson about challenge, "People arrive in all states. Happy, frustrated, tired. Some are demanding; some are nice. I like the challenge of figuring out how to relate to them and make them feel good about the hotel. The training helped me do that better." Mario thanked me. I was the one who took the most away from our work together.

One way to think about the People Equation is that getting the People Equation right is a starting point. Hire the most eligible and suitable people you can find for your job and then help them stretch and develop to unlock more of their potential.

In my work as an executive coach, I have been privileged to coach top performers in business. I never stop being amazed by their ability to learn and grow and take their performance to new levels; to turn resistance into enjoyment and develop their strengths.

So how can you have more Marios on your team? What does it take for you to tap into your people's capacity to take their performance to the next level? It starts by developing a growth mindset. Just as people with a value mindset look for what's going right, people with a growth mindset look for potential for growth. Once you identify a potential area for growth, find a way to give the person an opportunity to develop it. It's no different than the mindset good parents have in regard to their children. When a parent sees strength in a child, it is natural to look for a way to develop that strength. You look for the right school, ballet teacher or sports coach. You look for activities the child can engage in that will give the child an opportunity to stretch. It's just the same in business.

Practice 5: Fun

"It's tough, but it's fun." David Ogilvy actually promised "fun" as part of the work experience at Ogilvy & Mather. Fast forward 45 years to 2008. Google tops the *Fortune* magazine list of the 100 Best Companies to Work For. Larry Page of Google says, "Yes, you're going to work, but you're also going to have fun as well."[45]

There is a serious reason to have some fun at work. A growing body of research supports what Larry Page points to as common sense: "Happy people are more productive."[46]

Though it's really common sense, research shows that people are more engaged, creative and innovative when they are having fun. Injecting some fun can help relieve some of the stress that seems to be palpable in many organizations today. What's needed is the ability to strike a good balance between serious activity and fun—the ability to be serious or lighthearted as the situation requires. The ability to strike that balance is another aspect of good situational awareness. Katharine M. Hudson is an example of good situational awareness in the fun department.

"Try having some fun." That was Hudson's answer when she was asked how to energize a traditional manufacturing company that had been held back by turf battles, information hoarding and inflexibility. She gives that answer in a *Harvard Business Review* article she wrote in 2001 during her tenure as CEO of Brady Corporation.[47] She took the helm of a traditional Midwestern manufacturing company—so traditional that it didn't even allow employees to have coffee at their desks until 1989. She wrote the article seven years after first making fun part of the Brady Corporation culture. She points out that integrating fun as part of the culture was not an end in itself; rather, it was integrated for serious business reasons.

When Hudson took over as CEO in 1994, she wanted to stimulate a can-do atmosphere where people were open, collaborative and trusting. The cultural reality was that the Brady people tended to be uptight and cautious. To grow the business, she realized that she had to motivate people to loosen up and have some fun. So Hudson made having fun an important part of her strategy to grow the business. And she did grow the business—doubled sales and almost tripled net income and market capitalization in seven years. She certainly doesn't attribute that growth solely to having a fun culture. But she does emphasize that the business performance "is a sign that a company can be fun and friendly for its employees and fierce with its competitors." She believes that fun made the company fiercer "by making the organization more flexible and dynamic and our people more creative and enthusiastic."[48] Just like Larry Page, Hudson understood the connection between having fun and unlocking the creativity, innovation and enthusiasm that drive strong growth.

Humor and celebration—fun—are a natural part of life. Football stadiums erupt in cheers when the team scores! So do the players. Yeah, but we can't have that kind of exuberance at work. Why not? One reason I often hear is that it wouldn't be "professional." Being professional has somehow been construed to be synonymous with being "uptight"; that is being rigidly conventional and restrained in expressing emotion and humor. Rather, I'd suggest that being professional is about being able to be serious, humorous or exuberant as is appropriate for the situation. You can even have fun working in a bank!

I witnessed the impact of fun and camaraderie in a fast-growing community bank. The senior management of the bank believed that one of the major factors in the bank's success was that it was a great place to work. They had a core belief that how they treated their employees had a direct bearing on how their employees treated their customers. Importantly, they had also been very successful in recruiting top performers from competitors based on the bank's reputation as a great place to work. Senior management was concerned that the bank was losing some of its camaraderie, cheerfulness and gusto in the wake of aggressive growth. They enlisted me in their efforts to ensure that the bank remained a great place to work as it continued to grow in number of employees and locations. As we talked, they expressed concern that some employees were beginning to stress out more as the bank grew.

I suggested that management form a committee that included a cross-section of managers and rank-and-file from the various departments in the bank as well as various branch locations. The committee was charged with coming up with ways to preserve the culture—figure out how to continue to have fun and camaraderie in the middle of aggressive growth. The committee came up with great ways to promote fun and camaraderie.

The bank ended up making the committee a standing committee. I wanted to call it the "Committee on Fun," but the bank called it the "Culture Committee"—well, they are bankers. But they are bankers who have fun! For them, like the Brady Corporation, fun is not an end in itself; it is a means to attract and retain top talent and grow the business. It has proven to be a valuable recruiting tool for the bank. Every candidate is told that the bank has a standing committee that meets regularly to make sure that the bank remains a great place to work. The bank has consciously developed its motivational competency around fun and camaraderie.

If fostering fun is not in your personal comfort zone, you can still implement this management practice—still have motivational competency in this area. The bank's use of a committee is instructive: senior management "delegated" fun. What is important is that they made it clear that they were committed—that it was an important endeavor—and they supported the effort with the resources to make it successful. They truly empowered a fun culture.

Fun is another exercise of situational awareness. Certainly we all need to act appropriately. Granted, humor can be offensive or celebration inappropriate. But that does not mean that it is wise to throw the proverbial baby out with the bath water. Both collegiate and professional football officials, for instance, penalize "illegal celebration." The concept here is to define what is either appropriate or inappropriate for your culture—it's subjective—and then communicate the standards to your people. In the final analysis, instilling "appropriate" humor and fun into your culture is motivating.

Formula for Success

In short, the formula for success is to select people with high performance potential and then retain them. We have discussed five management practices that support a good retention strategy: fair compensation, appreciation, communication, providing an opportunity to stretch and grow and promoting fun. You will be able to both implement a good retention strategy and create a great place to work by routinely following these practices. You'll also save some bucks. There are various estimates of the cost of replacing an employee; the estimates range from several thousand dollars up to three times the employee's salary—not to mention the loss of productivity.

Culture definitely matters in getting and keeping the best talent. Like the bank mentioned earlier, Southwest Airlines—

long noted for an energizing culture—has a culture committee; it actually has two. I like what Gary Kelly, Southwest's current CEO, wrote in a *Spirit Magazine* column. He shared that Southwest tries to keep its culture "supportive, active and fun." That's a good formula for a successful culture.

If you get the right people for the job, they don't need to be managed as much as coached. Legendary basketball coach John Wooden teaches us that the ability to analyze and motivate talent is an important determinant of success. Coach Wooden won seven national basketball championships in a row, and yet he says that there is no area of basketball where he is a genius. Where was he really good? He said he was really good at motivating his players.[49] He attracted players with a lot of natural talent. The People Equation shows you how to identify people with the natural talent for your job. Coach Wooden was able to motivate his players to help them fulfill their full potential. By following the five management practices that foster motivational competency, you will be able to motivate your employees to fulfill their full potential.

Concluding Thoughts

I OPENED THIS BOOK at a dinner meeting where we were talking about a hiring mistake. I'd like to end it with a breakfast meeting where we were talking about a very different outcome. I had an early morning meeting with Bill, the founder-CEO of a construction-related company. He was happy to tell me that he had just given Andrew, the company's CFO, a very attractive ownership interest in the business. He was happy to tell me that because, several years before, there was doubt that Andrew would make it. I'd like to share with you how the People Equation factored into Andrew's turn-around success. It's an interesting story.

Bill wanted Andrew to succeed. He told me that "good things happened" when he could get Andrew focused on strategic problems. The difficulty for Bill was that Andrew always seemed stressed and overwhelmed with minutia, and it was hard to get him focused on strategic growth issues. Bill also had a problem with how Andrew was managing the upgrade of the company's information technology software. Bill had hoped Andrew could fast-track that project and spearhead future projects the company was planning in order to take the company to a new level of performance efficiency. Instead, the project seemed to be stalling out.

I was happy Bill was enlisting me in his efforts to get Andrew on track for success at the company. Two things needed to happen before I could engage with Andrew. First, Bill had to exercise a little motivational competency. As discussed earlier, communication is one of the management practices that create motivational competency. One dimension of communication we discussed is communicating about performance on a regular or timely basis. That was not one of Bill's competencies. Bill had not actually told Andrew that there were problems with his performance, much less that the problems were reaching a boiling point. Ouch! First step, communicate the problems to Andrew. Although Bill anticipated it being a difficult conversation—and it certainly could have been—Andrew was actually appreciative. He was glad to know where he stood and was open to Bill's offer to work with me.

By the way, Bill's failure to communicate with Andrew is not uncommon. Many—maybe even most—of us find it uncomfortable to give negative performance feedback. Delaying only allows the problems to build up. There is a greater risk that it will be a difficult conversation if you don't communicate performance problems early.

The second step that needed to happen was to get job suitability data—assessment data—on Andrew. However, the company had no experience with assessment tools. Bill had the same healthy skepticism that I actually had when I filled out my first assessment questionnaire. I asked Bill to be a guinea pig and fill out a Harrison Assessment questionnaire. His skepticism turned into support after we reviewed his report. Once Bill was on board with the assessment, Andrew also completed an assessment questionnaire.

I am clearly a strong advocate for using assessment tools and encourage you to do so when making talent decisions. Following the criteria set out at the beginning of the Assessment Technology section of this book will help you select the assesessment that best suits your company's strategic objectives and culture. Skepticism from someone with no experience with assessments is understandable. There is no better way to gain confidence in an assessment than to try it out on yourself.

What did Andrew's suitability data reveal? It showed that Andrew had the qualities that generally result in good strategic judgment—one of the things Bill most valued about Andrew. Andrew shared traits common to high-performing CFOs across industries. Traits like high self-motivation, strong analytics, attention to details, good adaptability, good interpersonal skills and a good balance between being authoritative and collaborative. Although he was generally well-suited for the job, there were several tendencies that appeared to contribute to his performance challenges. The assessment showed a strong tendency to be both permissive and self-sacrificing and suggested that Andrew didn't like planning. After he had reviewed the data, Andrew told me that the assessment was dead-on—his wife thought so too.

I asked Andrew if he agreed with Bill that he often seemed overwhelmed. He said, "I don't just seem overwhelmed, I am overwhelmed." As we explored why he was overwhelmed, it became clear that he was constantly dealing with errors his staff made or problems that he had to solve because a member of his staff had not fully thought through the issues. In short, he was being permissive with his staff and then doing a lot of the work himself to correct mistakes. He was ultimately sacrificing his personal well-being to compensate for the poor performance of his staff. Although it seemed clear to both of us that Andrew's permissiveness was intensifying the problem, the root cause was actually poor performance by the staff. Just like Bill, Andrew needed to develop some motivational competency around communication. He had "urged" people to do better, but had not enforced any consequences for poor performance. Rather, he personally picked up the slack. Andrew needed to clearly communicate where there were problems as well as the consequences of not improving.

Andrew began to hold his staff accountable. He started by defining the numerator in the People Equation: job activities, expected outcomes and how performance would be measured. He then *communicated* the activities, outcomes and measures to his staff. Everyone was on the same page regarding what was expected. One of the measures was error-free reporting from his staff. No one could really argue that it was always the expectation for the job; they had just not been delivering that result.

Like Bill—and I think most committed managers—Andrew wanted his people to succeed. He wanted to give them every chance he could to succeed—to measure up to the performance standards of the job. He shared with them the value he believed he had gotten from the assessment and made it available to anyone who wanted that kind of insight. He also made it clear that it would be for their professional development only. Their performance would strictly be judged by the performance measures he had communicated to them. Most of the staff wanted to fill out an assessment questionnaire. It was clear from the data that the joy factor was missing for most of them. They were in an administrative job, but did not enjoy activities that required attention to detail and really did not enjoy clerical work. Unfortunately, the nonnegotiable activities in the job were clerical in nature and required a strong attention to detail to avoid errors. I had great compassion for these folks. They were in much the same situation I described earlier when I was practicing law. Because I don't like highly detailed—or administrative—activities I had to put my nose to the grindstone. Even though you can be successful at things you don't like doing, grinding out performance takes a lot of energy. As noted earlier, people tend to perform better in a job where the majority of the activities—at least 75 percent—are activities they enjoy.

The pressure of grinding out work began to show as Andrew started holding his staff accountable. He stopped correcting the errors himself and, rather, sent them back to the person responsible. Within a couple of months, two members of the staff found other jobs and resigned. One of those people told him that sending all the work back was just creating too much pressure for her. When those two employees left, another employee asked if she could be reassigned to different job in the company. She had identified an available job for which she believed she was much better suited. Her assessment data confirmed that she was better suited for the other position. Andrew and the manager of the other position agreed to the transfer. That meant that Andrew would be replacing the core of his staff.

Andrew looked for people who were both eligible and suitable when replacing his staff. He found people who enjoyed administrative activities and who were detail oriented. He effectively worked the denominator of the People Equation. As a result, the huge volume of daily errors he had been dealing with began to evaporate. **Right person, right job, huge impact.** This time, Andrew clearly communicated expectations up front. His daily state of being inundated and overwhelmed began to evaporate as the volume of errors began to evaporate—as the new people began to meet performance measures.

I certainly don't want to sugarcoat the transition of Andrew's staff. Although it was worthwhile, it was definitely hard on them and hard on Andrew. In our early conversations Andrew agreed that he tended to be permissive with his staff—and probably in life generally. He explained that he did not want to be "a hard-ass." He now realized that in order to avoid being a hard-ass he was overcompensating by being permissive. And that had created the current problems. What was needed was the ability to strike a balance. As Roger Fisher and William Ury say in their book on negotiation, *Getting to Yes*, it is important to have the ability to "Be hard on the problem, soft on the people."[50] Andrew worked to develop his ability to strike that balance. Although it was uncomfortable, he persisted because he could see the value to himself and the company.

That didn't solve Andrew's whole problem. There was still the issue of managing projects. Consistent with the assessment data, he acknowledged that he didn't like planning and had not developed particularly good skills in that area. As he thought through the problem, he came to the conclusion that the project wasn't stalling out because he was resisting doing the work. Rather, he just wasn't confident that he really knew how to develop a good project plan. He believed it was an eligibility issue. It's an example of the cause and effect dynamic between suitability and eligibility. As Enjoyment Performance Theory explains, when we enjoy and activity—are suited for it—we tend to do it more often with the effect of getting better because we tend to get better at any activity as we do it more; we develop better eligibility with experience. On the other hand, if we don't like doing something—are not naturally suited for it—we tend to try to avoid it. Avoidance does not promote good eligibility.

Andrew called me one day after thinking about it to tell me that he had enrolled in a project management course at a local university. A couple of weeks into the course he knew that taking the course was the right thing to do. Applying what he was learning helped him get the project moving. As he started feeling more confident in his ability and got some success, to his surprise, he began to enjoy planning activities. Project management has now become a strength rather than a liability. It's not an uncommon alchemy. Alchemy is a medieval chemical philosophy that aimed at turning base metals into gold. Investing the time and discipline to master an activity can change resistance into joy. That seems to happen when experience creates a new, and more positive, perspective on an activity. I have enjoyed watching the many instances where talent has emerged as resistance to an activity has dissolved. On the other hand, experience may just reinforce why you don't like to do it. And that's also important to know

Back to my breakfast with Bill. He said Andrew had become an "ace" at managing a project. He started calling Andrew the "on time, on budget man." He was giving Andrew an interest in the company because he was now so valuable.

Andrew's is a story about someone who was at risk of losing his job because his staff lacked suitability and he resisted holding them accountable. He was suited for his job except for a tendency to be permissive. He wanted to avoid being a "hard-ass," so he overcompensated and failed to hold people accountable. As he addressed that tendency in himself, good things happened. He clearly defined the job—activities, outcomes and measures. Just as Bill had done with him, Andrew gave his people a chance to succeed. When they selected out of the job, he was able to get the right people (people who were eligible and suitable) into the job. And he developed his situational awareness—how he handled his relationship with others. He developed the ability to be "hard on the problem, soft on the people." He also recognized a need to improve his eligibility—his knowledge—in how to manage projects. The result was that Andrew realized the potential that Bill had seen in him when he was hired!

That breakfast was clearly a much better experience than the dinner story that I shared at the beginning of the book.

It also answers the question: is there a way to add logic, rigor and strategic depth to hiring and promoting decisions? There is. It's called the People Equation.

$$\frac{\text{Key Job Activities}}{(\text{Eligibility} + \text{Suitability})} = \text{High Performance Potential}$$

Some of the toughest decisions anyone makes in business are people decisions. Most people are committed to getting the right people in the right jobs—hiring highly talented people. The problem is that implementation is challenging because most of us have not been trained in how to assess talent. We genuinely think we are hiring a high performer only to be disappointed once the person is on board. As Peter Drucker observed: "The ability to make good decisions regarding people represents one of the last reliable sources of competitive advantage since very few organizations are very good at it."[51] My hope is that the People Equation will give you the implementation guidance you need to determine whether a person is the right person for the job. Following the People Equation's six steps for getting the right person in the right job will give you the guidance you need to build a talent advantage in your company.

The following summarizes the six steps:

Step 1: Identify nonnegotiable job activities

Really understand the job. Craft a strategic job description that captures the outcomes you want and the activities that must be done to achieve those outcomes— the nonnegotiable activities. As a leader, be hands-on. Define the nonnegotiable activities for your "A" positions: the mission critical jobs that have a major impact on customer satisfaction, efficiency, liability and/or profit.

Step 2: Define measurements for the activities

By establishing measurements for job activities you create clear performance expectations. Don't we all want to know that we are working on the right activities and what success looks like for those activities? It's also assured that what gets measured gets done.

Step 3: Establish eligibility requirements

Eligibility means that you have the education, skill and experience needed to do a job—that you can do it. Going through the process of defining optimum eligibility is important. Thinking through the level of education, training, skill and experience that will best promote success in the job gives you the most complete insight into a person's eligibility.

Step 4: Define and assess for suitability

Suitability means that you have the inherent traits and qualities that help you excel in a job. People who are well-suited for a job enjoy at least 75 percent of the activities in the job. They have the joy factor. They also have good situational awareness: they can respond effectively to the situations presented by the job. Advances in assessment technology can give you essential data on suitability traits. Assessment technology can give you insight into your secret sauce—the suitability traits that are shared by top performers in your company. Assessment data can also tell you if a person has the balance of traits that create good situational awareness or if there is a risk of counter-productive behavior.

Step 5: Strike the right balance between eligibility and suitability

Remember the scale sitting on a desk? One side of the scale is eligibility and the other side is suitability. For highly technical positions that require a lot of education and training, like doctors, the scale is heavily tipped toward eligibility. For jobs like product sales and customer service, the scale is heavily tipped toward suitability. For sales of services the scale is going to be more balanced. Why? Because when you sell something that is invisible you need a solid level of skill and experience to build trust in a customer or client. If you are selling a technical service, the scale is going to tip slightly toward eligibility. If you are selling a nontechnical service, the scale is going to tip slightly toward suitability.

Step 6: Conduct a structured interview

Planning for an interview delivers better results. We all have a tendency to fall into like very easily. It's so common it has a name: the halo effect. The halo effect happens when one good aspect of a candidate— for instance likability—makes the candidate look good in other areas without specific information about that area. Structure your interview to avoid the halo effect. Five tips for conducting a successful interview include:

1. Know what you are looking for.
2. Ask better questions. Ask situational, behavioral and introspective questions.
3. Interview your top performers.
4. Evaluate the joy factor.
5. Finally, check the halo.

Following the People Equation's six steps for getting the right person in the right job will improve your ability to make good people decisions. You then have the challenge of keeping the people you hire. A key to retention is to hire people who can do the job, who want to do the job and who want to do the job for you and your company. You need motivational competency to keep people once you hire them. Hire people with high performance potential and motivate them to achieve their full potential. That's the formula for success.

High Performance Potential

+ Motivation

Job Success

I have found that the following five management practices build motivational competency and result in employee satisfaction, a good working environment and strong culture:

Practice 1: Compensation

For most people compensation is not just about the amount of pay. It's about being satisfied with their pay. There is a strong connection between satisfaction with pay and fairness. For instance, people need to believe that they are paid on par with what other companies pay for similar work and what other employees of the company are paid.

Practice 2: Appreciation

Appreciation in business is one of the most powerful ways to motivate employees to give you their best. Lack of appreciation or recognition is one of the major reasons people quit their jobs. Start looking for what your people are doing well and share with them what you see. Be sincere and be timely in your appreciation. Appreciate both group performance and individual performance.

Practice 3: Communication

Candid communication—keeping people in the loop— is important all of the time and essential during a crisis. Masters of motivational competency also clearly communicate performance expectations, communicate about performance on a regular basis and listen.

Practice 4: Opportunity to Stretch and Grow

We are all born with an innate desire to grow and develop. Provide employees with opportunities to stretch and achieve in their work environment—and provide them with the training necessary to stretch and grow.

Practice 5: Fun

Though it's really common sense, research shows that people are more engaged, creative and innovative when they are having fun. Make fun part of your growth strategy.

David Ogilvy saw culture as a competitive advantage—the thing that more than anything else differentiated his company from its competitors. Mastering motivational competency—consistently implementing the five managerial practices—will help you build the kind of culture that differentiates you from your competitors and helps you realize a sustainable talent advantage. Motivational competency helps you tap into performance potential and promote job success.

I worked out the People Equation to help myself and my clients make better people decisions because, frankly, as Peter Drucker observed, we were not really very good at it. Certainly not as good as with other business-related decisions. Systematically applying the People Equation has helped us, and I'm confident it will also help you as well. My aspiration in writing this book is that you will be better able to get the right people in the right jobs and keep them by creating a great place to work. I wish you success in your people decisions.

APPENDIX

Job Activities Worksheet

Nonnegotiable Job Activities

Job: _____

- What outcomes do you expect from the job?

- What job activities are nonnegotiable—must be done to achieve the outcomes you want?

1. (Job activity)
   - How will you measure the activity?

2. (Job activity)
   - How will you measure the activity?

3. (Job activity)
   - How will you measure the activity?

4. (Job activity)
   - How will you measure the activity?

APPENDIX

Sample Job Description

Example of a job description created by the General Manager for a manufacturing company:

1.0 INTRODUCTION

1.1 The purpose of this job description is to establish and define the eligibility requirements, principal duties (non-negotiable activities) and performance standards for the Operations Manager for the Bay City Operation of XYZ, Inc.

2.0 AUTHORITY

2.1 The Operations Manager receives authority directly from the V.P. of Regulation & Control Global Operations.

3.0 REPORTING RELATIONSHIPS

3.1 The Operations Manager reports directly to the V.P. of Regulation & Control Global Operations.

4.0 REQUIREMENTS FOR ELIGIBILITY

4.1 Education –

Required (Minimum)	4 year Bachelors Degree
Preferred (Optimum)	In addition to the above minimum requirements.... • Engineering or related Manufacturing Field

4.2 Licensing/Registration/Certification –

Required (Minimum)	None
Preferred (Optimum)	Prefer Six Sigma Certification

4.3 Experience –

Required (Minimum)	10 plus years in component and/or assembly manufacturing environment 3 years experience in direct supervision of both hourly and salary employees 3 years experience in managing of Production Planning and Purchasing personnel
Preferred (Optimum)	In addition to the items listed above: • 3 plus years in Natural Gas Industry or related field • Understanding of MRP systems • Understanding of Supplier Development systems • Managing experience and understanding of Quality and Manufacturing Engineering including lean manufacturing practices and 5S

4.4 Working Conditions—
Able to work in facility that is not air-conditioned. Work will be split between a climate-controlled office environment and the manufacturing area, which is heated in the winter but not cooled in the summer.

4.5 Work Time—
Able to work more than 40 hours weekly. Time in excess of 40 hours is the norm for this position. Manufacturing often will fabricate components and assemble products on weekends and holidays as dictated by business need, so support during these additional work days may be required.

4.6 Travel—
Able to do some travel. This position does not normally involve travel; however, business needs may necessitate some amount of travel to customers, suppliers, equipment manufacturers, corporate business activities, and training but should not be more than 10–15 percent annually.

5.0 PRINCIPAL DUTIES – NON NEGOTIABLE ACTIVITIES

5.1 Provide a safe and healthy manufacturing environment.

5.2 Lead the creation and execution of a production plan that, when executed successfully by manufacturing and purchasing, provides a product that meets a customer's quality and delivery expectations.

5.3 Manage to the safety, quality, delivery and cost objectives.

5.4 Manage RM, WIP and FG inventory to minimum levels that can still support the production plan.

5.5 Purchase and maintain equipment.

6.0 PERFORMANCE MEASUREMENTS

The Operations Manager shall be viewed as performing in an acceptable manner when the following results have occurred:

6.1 Leading indicator: Near-miss reporting and safety training meets objectives

Lagging indicator: RIR and Incident Severity meet annual targets

6.2 Leading indicator: Shop schedule attainment

Lagging indicator: Customer OTD to Promise and COQ KPI target are met

6.3 Leading indicator: Part shortages and visual inventory indicators

Lagging indicator: Inventory turns and E&O

6.4 Leading indicator: Part shortages, supplier audit scores

Lagging indicator: Supplier rejects, Supplier OTD, Supplier Cost reductions

6.5 Leading indicator: On-time PM

Lagging indicator: Equipment down time, number of emergency repairs

Endnotes

1. Heskett, James L., Sasser, W. Earl and Schlesinger, Leonard A., *The Service Profit Chain, How Leading Companies Link Profit and Growth to Loyalty, Satisfaction and Value,* The Free Press, 1997, p. 116

2. Dan Harrison, Ph.D. is an international leader in behavioral assessments. He has over 30 years of experience and a diverse background in mathematics, personality theory, counseling psychology, human potential psychology, and organizational psychology. Dr. Harrison's involvement in human potential psychology led to his creation of the Harrison Assessment™, an assessment instrument based on over 20 years of job performance research that helps companies get the right person in the right job.

3. Roman, Kenneth, "The House That Ogilvy Built," *Strategy + Business,* Issue 54, Spring 2009, p. 30

4. Roman, p. 30

5. Drucker, Peter F., *The Effective Executive,* Harper & Row, 1967, p. 80

6. Bossidy, Larry and Charan, Ram, *Execution, the Discipline of Getting Things Done,* Crown Business, 2002, p. 113

7. Labovitz, George and Rosansky, Victor, *The Power of Alignment, How Great Companies Stay Centered and Accomplish Extraordinary Things,* John Wiley & Sons, Inc., 1997, Fred Smith is quoted on p. 6

8. Huselid, Mark A., Beatty, Richard W. and Becker, Brian

E., "'A Players' or 'A Positions'? The Strategic Logic of Workforce Management,'" *Harvard Business Review*, December, 2005, reprint R0512G, p. 2

9. Huselid, p. 24

10. Boudreau, John W. and Ramstad, Peter M., "Talentship and the Evolution of Human Resource Management: From 'Professional Practices' to 'Strategic Talent Decision Science,'" *CEO Publication* G 04-6 (458), 2004, p. 13

11. Boudreau, p. 13

12. Govern, Paul, "Demystifying Malpractice Risk," *Reporter, Vanderbilt Medical Center's Weekly Newspaper*, 4/26/2002

13. Beckwith, Harry, *Selling the Invisible, A Field Guide to Modern Marketing*, Warner Books, 1997, p. xvi

14. Flannery, William J., *The Lawyer's Field Guide to Effective Business Development*, ABA Publishing, 2007, p. 15

15. Flannery, p. 2

16. Harrison, Dan, http://www.harrisonassessments.com/enjoyment-performance.html

17. Buckingham, Marcus and Clifton, Donald O., *Now, Discover Your Strengths*, The Free Press, 2001, Warren Buffett is quoted p. 19

18. Hull, Billy, "Warriors' Rausch Has Tired Arm, Junior Greg Alexander Fills in as QB," *Honolulu Star-Bulletin*, Vol. 13, Issue 236, August 23, 2008

20. Cleary, Thomas F., translation of Sun Tzu, *The Art of War*, Shambahala Publications, Inc., 1988, p. 53

21. Center for Creative Leadership, *A Look at Derailment Today: North America and Europe*, © 1996 Center for Creative Leadership, all rights reserved, pp. 2, 6, 8 and 9

22. Center for Creative Leadership, p. 16

23. Tropman, John E., *The Management of Ideas in the Creating Organization*, Greenwood Publishing Group, 1998, p. 84

24. Center for Creative Leadership, p. 68

25. Collins, Jim, *Good to Great, Why Some Companies Make the Leap . . . and Others Don't*, HarperCollins Publishers, 2001, p. 39

26. Collins, p. 36

27. Collins, p. 22

28. Cialdini, Robert B., *Influence Science and Practice*, Fourth Edition, Allyn and Bacon, 2001, p. 176

29. Roman, p. 30

30. Roman, p. 4

31. Roman, p. 5

32. Edmans, Alex, *Does the Stock Market Fully Value Intangibles? Employee Satisfaction and Equity Prices*, Wharton School, University of Pennsylvania, June 1, 2010, p. 25, http://w4.stern.nyu.edu/salomon/docs/conferences/edmans.pdf

33. Heath, Chip, "On the Social Psychology of Agency Relationships: Lay Theories of Motivation Overemphasize Extrinsic Incentives," *Organizational Behavior and*

Human Decision Processes, Vol. 78, No. 1, April, 1999, pp. 33–39

34. Sirota, David, Mischkind, Louis and Meltzer, Michael, *The Enthusiastic Employee, How Companies Profit by Giving Workers What They Want*, Wharton School Publishing, 2005, pp. 79–80

35. Sirota, p. 83

36. Gostick, Adrian and Elton, Chester, *The Carrot Principle, How the Best Managers Use Recognition to Engage Their People, Retain Talent and Accelerate Performance*, Free Press, 2007, p. 9

37. Gostick, pp. 15–19

38. Gostick, p. 18

39. Guilmartin, Nance, *The Power of Pause, How to Be More Effective in a Demanding 24/7 World*, Jossey-Bass, 2010, p. 48

40. Blanchard, Kenneth and Johnson, Spencer, *The One Minute Manager*, William Morrow and Company, Inc., 1981, 1982, p. 39

41. Welch, Jack and Suzy, "Morale Up in a Downturn," http://www.businessweek.com/magazine/content/08_18/b4082080038715.htm

42. Opinion Research Corporation, March 5, 2009 press release, http://www.opinionresearch.com/fileSave%5CEmployee_OuchPoint_FinalMarch042009.pdf

43. Skinner, Fran and Ziegler, Jamie, *Investment Leadership and Employee Engagement in 2010. The Impact of the '08-*

'09 Financial Crisis on Investment Firm Culture and How Leaders are Responding, p. 10, AUMPartners' White Paper, 2010. AUMPartners provides research and consulting to investment firms.

44. Cordin, Ed, and others. *$37 Billion: Counting the Cost of Employee Misunderstanding,* IDC White Paper, June, 2008, http://www.cognisco.com/downloads/white-paper/uk_exec_sumamry.pdf. IDC is a global provider of market intelligence.

45. *Fortune,* "100 Best Places to Work," http://money.cnn.com/magazines/fortune/bestcompanies/2007/snapshots/1.html

46. Lashinsky, Adam, "Back2Back Champs," *Fortune,* February 4, 2008, Vol. 157, No. 2, p. 70

47. Hudson, Katherine M., "Transforming a Conservative Company—One Laugh at a Time," *Harvard Business Review,* July–August, 2001

48. Hudson, p. 11

49. Wooden, Coach John, and Jamison, Steve, *Wooden, A Lifetime of Observations and Reflections on and Off the Court,* McGraw Hill, 1977, p. 113

50. Fisher, Roger and Ury, William, *Getting to Yes, Negotiating Agreement Without Giving In,* Penguin Books, 1993, p. 54

51. Smith, Bradford and Smart, Geoffrey, "Topgrading the Organization," *Directors and Boards,* Spring, 1997

Harrison Assessment and Paradox Technology are trademarks owned by Harrison Assessments Int'l Ltd.

About the Author

Logan Loomis provides consulting, coaching and training to companies to help them unlock performance potential in their business and in their people. He helps companies get the right people in the right jobs and keep them. Logan began his career as a corporate lawyer for a prominent New Orleans law firm. He moved into private enterprise after a decade practicing law. He led sales and marketing efforts as Vice President of Sales and Marketing for LEDCO, Inc., a natural gas pipeline company then listed by *Inc.* magazine as one of the 100 fastest growing companies in America. He was CEO of Nortech Energy Corp., a natural gas trading and marketing joint venture of a large diversified energy company.

Clients routinely call on Logan to help them identify, develop and retain high-performing salespeople. He provides sales and negotiation training based on his primer *Both Sides Win, The 3 Secrets for Success in Customer Negotiation.*

Logan holds a BA degree from the University of Texas, Austin, Texas and a Juris Doctor degree from Southern Methodist University, Dallas, Texas.

CPSIA information can be obtained at www.ICGtesting.com
Printed in the USA
BVOW030833061011

272919BV00001B/22/P